D1617464

Books by Richard Headstrom

Adventures with Freshwater Animals
Adventures with Insects
Adventures with a Hand Lens
Adventures with a Microscope

ADVENTURES WITH FRESHWATER ANIMALS

Adventures with

by Richard Headstrom

ILLUSTRATED BY THE AUTHOR

FRESHWATER ANIMALS

J. B. LIPPINCOTT COMPANY
Philadelphia and New York

TO MY WIFE

CONTENTS

INTRODUCTION   *11*

ADVENTURE

1   *We Meet the First Animals*   *13*

2   *We Undertake Some Experiments*   *16*

3   *We Perform Some Further Experiments*   *20*

4   *We Seek an Upside-down Animal*   *26*

5   *We Watch an Animal Turn Cartwheels*   *30*

6   *We Encounter the Springtails*   *38*

7   *We Examine the Bottom Mud of Trashy Pools*   *40*

8   *We Explore Shallow Riffles*   *41*

9   *We Investigate Jet Propulsion*   *44*

10 *We See a Stick That Moves*   *47*

11 *We Play Nursemaid*   *49*

12 *We Become Acquainted with Some Clams and Mussels*   *57*

13 *We Look into a Roadside Ditch*   *65*

14 *We Visit an Animal Garden*   *67*

15 *We Climb among the Rocks of a Waterfall*   *73*

16 *We Observe an Unusual Event*   *76*

17 *We Solve a Mystery*   *83*

18 *We Get to Know the Mayflies*   *87*

19 *We Hear Some Unusual Voices*   *91*

20 *We Do Some Grafting*   *99*

21 *We Make a Surprising Discovery*   *109*

22	*We Gather a Few Snails*	*111*
23	*We Peek into a Roadside Puddle*	*119*
24	*We Ask a Question*	*124*
25	*We Spy on the Sunfish*	*129*
26	*We Learn about Countershading*	*132*
27	*We Study Some Worms*	*134*
28	*We Capture Some Water Mites*	*138*
29	*We Are Deceived*	*141*
30	*We Attend a Ritual*	*143*
31	*We Catch Some Giants*	*150*
32	*We Venture into Animal Husbandry*	*152*
33	*We Inspect Some Examples of Insect Architecture*	*158*
34	*We Test the Behavior of the Crayfish*	*164*
35	*We Are Intrigued by the Water Fleas*	*169*
36	*We Come upon the Unexpected*	*176*
37	*We Are Introduced to an Efficiency Expert*	*178*
38	*We Discover an Incongruity*	*183*
39	*We Are Captivated by the Antics of the Scuds*	*185*
40	*We Hunt the Water Tigers*	*187*
41	*We Engage in a Matter of Identification*	*191*
42	*We Quest for the One-eyed Cyclops*	*195*
43	*We Turn Our Attention to the Ostracods*	*198*
44	*We Intrude on the Privacy of the Wheel Animalcules*	*201*
45	*We Marvel at Nature's Ingenuity*	*206*
46	*We Acquire Some Pets*	*209*
47	*We Arrive at the End of the Book*	*214*

VISIT the nearest pond or stream or the brooklet that winds its way through the countryside and you will find such places teeming with life. Even a temporary woodland pool or a puddle along the roadside has its own animal population.

What do you know of the animals that live in our fresh waters, their habits, their behavior? If you are of an inquiring mind, are interested in the outdoors, and want to know more of the world you live in, come with me on the following adventures. Some of you may even be stimulated to carry on research of your own, for there is much we do not know. What is also important, no elaborate or expensive equipment is needed, with the exception of a microscope, which is necessary for a few of the adventures and is now within the price range of all. What you will need can be found around the house or may be made with little effort. Without further preamble let us turn to the first adventure, which deals, and rightly so, with the first animals.

11

We Meet the First Animals

SINCE first things should come first, we shall begin our series of adventures with the first animals, scientifically known as the protozoa, from the Greek roots *proto,* first, and *zoa,* animals.

The protozoa are minute primitive animals and structurally represent a unit mass of protoplasm, the living substance of which plants and animals are composed; in other words they are one-celled animals. Most of them live a solitary existence, although a few live in groups of cells and are known as colonial protozoans. These colonial protozoans include certain plantlike organisms that for years have posed the problem of whether they are actually plants or animals. They are borderline cases exhibiting both animal- and plant-like characteristics.

Although a few protozoans may be seen with the naked eye or hand lens, they are essentially microscopic in size and, to observe them, you will need a microscope.

In spite of their small size protozoans are capable of carrying on all the processes neces-

Figure 1
CHILOMONAS

sary to living. They capture their food, digest it, and convert it to protoplasm for growth and repair. They take in oxygen to oxidize their food materials for heat and energy with which to carry on their activities, and they expel the waste products of metabolism, the sum of the processes involved in the building up and breaking down of protoplasm, as well as undigested food materials. They also move about by various means and of course are capable of reproducing their kind. They even respond to stimuli, as we shall see. Basically they are, therefore, much like ourselves except that we are much more complex and consist of millions of cells that have become differentiated. These different kinds of cells form tissues that in turn form organs designed to carry on a particular activity. Among the protozoa each animal is a solitary and free-living organism capable of existing by itself and performing all the operations necessary to existence and survival. However, in the colonial forms some cells have become differentiated for reproductive purposes, and thus we have division of labor, characteristic of all higher animals. Some of these colonial forms serve as a link between the protozoa, the one-celled animals, and the metazoa, the many-celled animals.

Where can we find protozoans? Every pool,

Figure 2
COLPIDIUM

brook, pond, stream, and lake has its population of these simple animals. To collect them, we can use anything with which we can scoop up water—an old pan, for instance. We also take some of the bottom mud, a few dead leaves floating in the water or lying on the bottom, and a few dead twigs or sticks if they are present, as well as a few submerged water plants. The water we scoop up as well as all these other materials we place in some clean jars or bottles.

On returning home we examine our "catch." The procedure merely involves transferring a drop of water to a microscope slide, covering the drop with a cover slip, and examining with a microscope. We take samples of water from various levels in the jars, as some species are surface forms, others are bottom dwellers, and still others swim about at various depths. We also examine a little of the mud and scrapings from the surfaces of the leaves, twigs, and sticks, as some species haunt such places.

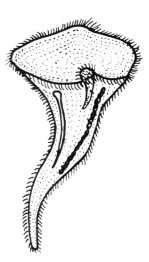

Figure 3
STENTOR

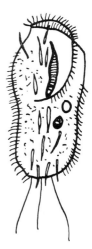

Figure 6
STYLONCHIA

Figure 4
BLEPHARISMA

Figure 5
MONAS

What species should we expect to find? I have pictured some of the commoner forms in Figures 1 to 6. As you watch these animals move about under the microscope in an area no larger than a drop of water, you will be fascinated and amazed at what you see.

ADVENTURE 2

We Undertake Some Experiments

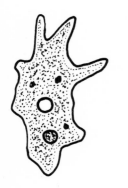

Figure 7
AMOEBA

MERELY to observe the protozoa, especially for the first time, is a rewarding experience, but we can make our observations more definitive by doing a few simple experiments. Let us first concentrate on a search for the amoeba (Figure 7), which can usually be obtained from the scrapings of a submerged leaf. Under the microscope it appears as an irregular, grayish particle of animated jelly that is continually changing its shape by thrusting out and withdrawing little fingerlike processes called pseudopodia, which means false feet. By virtue of these pseudopodia the amoeba moves from place to place, captures other organisms, and ingests solid particles of food.

Watch an amoeba for a few moments and you will observe that the pseudopodia may arise at any point on the surface of the animal. Actually the amoeba moves along by thrusting out pseudopodia and then flowing into them. Although it appears a simple enough

16

process, we are still not sure how these false feet are formed.

What we are more interested in is how the amoeba captures its food and what happens to it. The amoeba feeds principally on minute animals and plants, but not every plant or animal that it encounters is ingested—the animal exercises a certain amount of selectivity. However, when it does come in contact with suitable food, the pseudopodia enclose the material, which is engulfed or ingested through the surface of the body. As soon as the food material is ingested, a temporary stomach, or food vacuole, is formed about the material and digestive fluids are then secreted into the vacuole. The entire process of food ingestion takes one or more minutes, depending on the character of the food and the temperature. Sometimes a dozen or so organisms may be engulfed and sometimes the amoeba may not be successful in accomplishing what it undertakes; at times it shows an astonishing amount of persistency generally found only in higher organisms.

To show that the amoeba is selective as to food, place it in a drop of water containing various other protozoans, such as Chilomonas (Figure 1), Colpidium (Figure 2), Stentor (Figure 3), Blepharisma (Figure 4), and Monas (Figure 5), and observe what happens. You will find that the animal will ingest some of these protozoans and reject others. You will also see that food vacuoles sometimes form of different colors, depending upon the food source, red with Blepharisma, green with Stentor. At times you may see the captured prey moving within the vacuole. Chilomonads, for instance, remain alive in the food vacuoles from three to nineteen minutes and are digested in from twelve to twenty-four hours.

Touch an amoeba with a small glass rod and you will find that it will cease to move for a time and then move slowly away (Figure 8). This reaction to a stimulus, in this case

glass rod   glass rod   glass rod

Figure 8
REACTIONS OF AMOEBA
TO TOUCH

touch or contact, is called a response. A response may be either positive or negative. The amoeba in moving away from the rod exhibits negative thigmotropism. The term thigmotropism is used in describing reaction to contact.

Next place a little salt, sugar, or vinegar in a drop of water containing an amoeba and

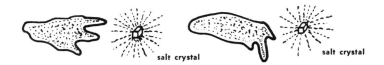

Figure 9
REACTIONS OF AMOEBA
TO A SALT CRYSTAL

observe that the amoeba will again show a negative reaction (negative chemotropism) (Figure 9). Try some other substances and you may find that it will show a positive reaction and result in ingestion. Next shine a strong light on the slide containing an amoeba and note that it will orient itself in respect to the direction of the rays and move away from it (negative phototropism) (Figure 10), but then try a weak light and you will probably find the amoeba moving toward it (positive photo-

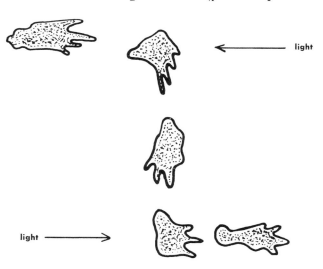

Figure 10
REACTIONS OF AMOEBA
TO A STRONG LIGHT

tropism). We have mentioned that temperature affects the rate of food taking. Gradually heat one end of the slide and the amoeba will move away from the stimulus; chill the slide sufficiently and the animal will cease to move.

ADVENTURE 3

We Perform Some Further Experiments

THE PARAMECIUM is as well known as the amoeba, if not more so. It has the distinction of being one of the first living things seen with the microscope, when it was invented in the seventeenth century. This protozoan, shown in Figure 11, is shaped somewhat like a slipper and is known as the slipper animalcule. It is abundant in ponds, and if you collect some pond water containing decayed plant material you should have no trouble securing a number of paramecia. As these animals show a positive response to gravity (positive geotropism) and swim up to the top of the collecting bottle, you should examine the water at the higher levels.

The paramecium is propelled through the water by fine protoplasmic processes, called cilia, that cover the body, but since they beat obliquely the animal rotates on its long axis as it swims forward (Figure 12). If you want to see how the cilia create a current of water, add a pinch of carmine powder (which you

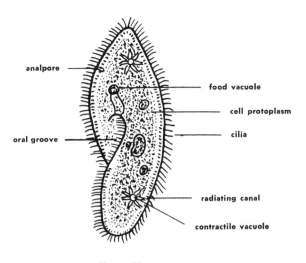

analpore

food vacuole

cell protoplasm

cilia

oral groove

radiating canal

contractile vacuole

Figure 11
PARAMECIUM

Figure 12
SPIRAL PATH OF
SWIMMING PARAMECIUM

can obtain at the drugstore). You may also observe the formation of a food ball in the oral groove, and the passage of the dark red food mass into the cell protoplasm, where a food vacuole is formed. If you are unable to get any carmine powder, substitute a drop of India ink; in this case the food vacuole will appear black.

Should you want to follow the process of digestion, obtain some yeast cells (get a yeast cake at the grocery store and break a small piece in water), stain them with Congo red (a red dye also obtainable at the drugstore), and place them near the animal. The yeast cells will be taken into the body, where a food vacuole will be formed. As you follow the

21

process of digestion you will note a change in the color of the Congo red to a blue green, which indicates that the vacuole has become acid. You will further note that the food vacuole circulates through the body or rather is carried about by the rotary streaming movement (cyclosis) of the protoplasm, and that it gradually changes back to a red-orange color, indicating that the vacuole and its contents have become less acid (Figure 13). Actually the vacuole and contents have become alkaline, although the red-orange color is no proof of this change, since the dye is an indicator of acid only. If you wish you can substitute a few drops of milk for the yeast cells and stain them with the same dye. Or you can try other substances and determine what the paramecia will accept or reject. You can also try to find out whether the paramecia will continue to take in carmine particles that they cannot digest, or will eventually "learn" to reject them.

Both the amoeba and the paramecium, as well as other protozoa, have structures called contractile vacuoles. Although these structures may serve in excretion, their primary function is to regulate the water content of the cell body. Water not only enters the body with the food but also enters through the general surface and is, furthermore, a by-

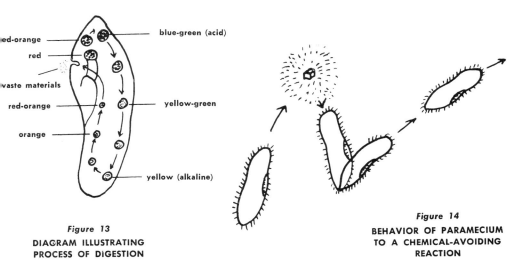

ed-orange

red

waste materials

red-orange

orange

blue-green (acid)

yellow-green

yellow (alkaline)

Figure 13
DIAGRAM ILLUSTRATING
PROCESS OF DIGESTION

Figure 14
BEHAVIOR OF PARAMECIUM
TO A CHEMICAL-AVOIDING
REACTION

product of oxidation. In the amoeba the contractile vacuole is formed as needed and any-
where in the body; in the paramecium two
contractile vacuoles are present, occupying
definite positions, one near each end of the
body. They communicate with a large portion
of the body by means of a system of radiating
canals. These canals fill with liquid, then discharge their contents to form the vacuole,
which in turn ejects the liquid to the exterior.
After each discharge a new vacuole is formed.
You can observe the rhythmic pulsations of
the vacuoles clearly by darkening the field.
Simply reduce the light by closing the dia-
phragm of your microscope a bit. If the paramecia and other ciliated protozoans you may
study move too fast, wait until the water has

23

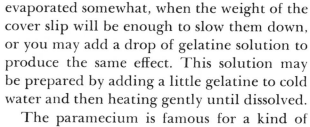

evaporated somewhat, when the weight of the cover slip will be enough to slow them down, or you may add a drop of gelatine solution to produce the same effect. This solution may be prepared by adding a little gelatine to cold water and then heating gently until dissolved.

The paramecium is famous for a kind of response to stimuli known as the avoiding reaction (Figure 14). Add a little chemical, such as a particle of salt, to the slide and observe what happens when the animal comes within reach of the dissolving salt. It will likely reverse its cilia and back up. At the same time it will slow down its rotating motion and swerve toward the aboral side, that is, the side opposite the oral groove. Then, using its posterior end as a sort of pivot, it will swing in a circle. Meanwhile some of the surrounding medium is being conveyed into the oral groove, and when it no longer contains the stimulus to which the animal reacts negatively, the cilia resume their normal beating and the paramecium moves forward again. Should its forward progress again bring it in contact with the harmful chemical, the avoiding reaction is repeated and as often as necessary until the animal no longer receives the stimulus to which it reacts negatively.

The paramecium reacts, not only to chemicals, but to contact, to changes in tempera-

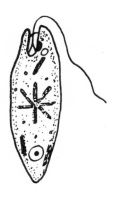

Figure 15
EUGLENA

24

ture, light, electricity, and other stimuli. You should be able to devise many experiments to test these responses, not only in the paramecium, but in other protozoans. Euglena (Figure 15), for instance, shows a positive response to light. You can readily observe this positive reaction by placing a number of these organisms in a finger bowl. Then cover the finger bowl with a card so that a bright light shining down on the dish falls on one half of the dish. Wait for ten minutes, remove the cover, and observe the concentration of euglenas in large numbers in the lighted half of the dish.

Large protozoans like Spirostomum (Figure 16) or Stentor (Figure 3) quickly respond to contact or disturbance, and this reaction may be observed by mounting a drop of water containing these organisms on a slide and tapping the slide. The organisms will immediately contract. You can observe this behavior with the naked eye, but, to watch the same response with Vorticella (Figure 17), a stalked form, you will need a microscope.

A most interesting experiment can be tried with Stentor. Drop a few carmine particles (obtainable at the drugstore) on the animal. The animal turns to one side. Now drop a few more particles on the animal from another direction. It changes its position, but since it

Figure 16
SPIROSTOMUM

Figure 17
VORTICELLA CONTRACTED
AND EXPANDED

25

cannot entirely escape the particles it reverses its cilia and attempts to blow them away. Not successful, it contracts within its protective tube. The animal has made several attempts to escape the carmine particles, and only one was effective. The question now is what will the animal do when it emerges and once again is subjected to the carmine particles? Will it repeat the entire cycle or will it immediately contract? You will find that the animal contracts as soon as the carmine particles touch it, which would suggest that the animal's behavior can be modified by experience.

ADVENTURE 4

We Seek an Upside-down Animal

IN LATE WINTER or early spring visit a pond or pool formed by melting snow or rainwater and look for an animal swimming on its back. You may have to visit several ponds or pools before you find it, for the presence of this animal in such places is not always assured, although it is common and widely distributed.

The animal is called the fairy shrimp (Figure 18). It is not a shrimp, though somewhat shrimplike in form, and is semitransparent with all the tints of the rainbow. It is an interesting animal and worth the time and energy spent in looking for it.

Fairy shrimps measure about an inch long,

brood pouch

Figure 18
FEMALE FAIRY SHRIMP

but they may reach a length of four inches. They are propelled through the water by eleven pairs of leaf-like appendages.* These appendages, or leaf feet, as they are called, are actually gill feet, since they serve as respiratory organs as well, and are provided with "chewing bases" that help manipulate the food. The gill feet are borne on the body segments posterior to the head, and in swimming each pair in succession from the hindmost forward is pressed back against the water. At the same time currents of water pass over the gills and convey to the mouth microscopic plants and animals on which the fairy shrimp feeds. When swimming the waving plumes of the gill-feet are the most conspicuous part of the animal and are a pleasing contrast to the rich body colors that shimmer in the light.

It is rather difficult to observe the fairy

Figure 19
NAUPLIUS OF FAIRY SHRIMP

---

* Fairy shrimps are scientifically called phyllopods and belong to a group known as the Phyllopoda, from the Greek meaning leaf-footed.

clasping organ

Figure 20
HEAD OF MALE SHOWING
CLASPING ORGAN

shrimp at close range in a pond or pool; to study the manner in which it swims, capture one or two specimens and take them home, where you can observe them to better advantage. Keep them in an aquarium, jar, dishpan, or a similar container, but be sure the temperature of the water is kept at about the same as that of the water in which you found them. Note that the hind part of the body is slender and without appendages and is brightly colored by the blood, red with hemoglobin. Sometimes the back is so transparent that you can see the pulsations of the long, tubular heart. Examine the gill-feet closely and you will find a flattened plate at a point near where they are attached to the body. This plate is used in breathing. You may also observe that the head is large and that the two black eyes are elevated on the ends of short stalks.

When the ice begins to break in spring, adults, spiderlike young (nauplii) (Figure 19) recently hatched from eggs, and maturing young, or larvae, may all be found swimming about in ponds or in temporary pools formed by melting snow or by rain. As this is the mating season, many mating pairs may be seen swimming about together, always on their backs, the male above the female in close embrace. The sexes may easily be distinguished, the male by his modified antennae, the female by the prominent brood pouch (Figure 18) on the abdomen. The modified antennae of the male, called claspers, which are used to hold the female, consist of an upper half, which is broad and thick, and a stiff, bristlelike prolongation, with a short bristlelike tooth on the inner side at the point where the two parts are connected (Figure 20). Just behind his gills, on the eleventh segment of the body, are the tubelike appendages by which he transfers the sperm cells to the female. You can see these appendages if you have collected a male.

Since fairy shrimps can live only in cold water, it is only a matter of several weeks before mating has been accomplished and as the water begins to warm up the adults begin to fall to the bottom to die. Meanwhile the females have produced resting eggs that also fall to the bottom, where they lie dormant either in the wet mud or the bottom mud of pools that dry up.

The eggs can resist long periods of desiccation. It appears necessary for the eggs to lie dormant for considerable periods, including the entire summer. As a matter of fact, some eggs even appear to need drying before they can hatch. Fairy shrimps have not been observed active through the summer, although

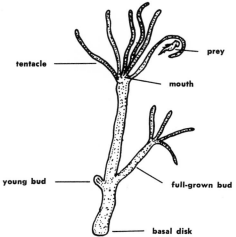

tentacle

prey

mouth

young bud

full-grown bud

basal disk

Figure 21
HYDRA

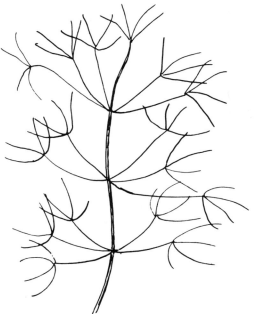

Figure 22
NITELLA

Figure 23
ELODEA, WATERWEED

they may be so in very cold water.

The eggs usually do not hatch until some-time in late winter. At that time they hatch into nauplii, which gradually acquire the typical appendages of the adults and become larvae, molting several times in the process. The larvae grow rapidly, becoming mature in six or seven days. In the average New England spring the fairy-shrimp population may reach its maximum within a week or two after the ice is off the ponds.

That the eggs are sensitive to temperature changes and are ready to develop by fall seems quite evident, for young fairy shrimps have been found in ponds during mild weather following a very early autumn freeze. However, the young observed were killed by the warm spells that followed. This may explain to some extent why the distribution of these animals is freakish and irregular, for in ponds where young were observed in the autumn few if any were seen the following spring. Thus fairy shrimps that may be found in ponds or pools for several years in succession may suddenly not appear at all, even though the conditions may seem to be right for them.

ADVENTURE 5

We Watch an Animal Turn Cartwheels

CAN YOU IMAGINE an animal moving from place to place by doing a series of cartwheels or somersaults? The hydra (Figure 21) occasionally uses this method of getting about. In Greek mythology the hydra was a nine-headed dragon slain by Hercules. There is a degree of similarity between the mythological monster and the hydra.

Hydras, which are our freshwater representative of the marine coelenterates—jellyfishes, sea anemones, and corals—are common in ponds, slow streams, and sunlit pools and are found throughout the year. You will find them hanging from plant stems like Nitella (Figure 22) and Elodea (Figure 23) or from the undersides of lily pads. Since they are small and difficult to observe in their natural habitat, it is best to transfer them to an

Figure 24
HYDRAS HANGING FROM PLANTS, SOME EXPANDED, SOME CONTRACTED

Figure 25
MYRIOPHYLLUM, WATER MILFOIL

aquarium of some sort. A battery jar or even a plain glass dish will do. In collecting hydras it is necessary to gather a few water plants as well as some water in which they were growing and let the plants and water stand for a while. If hydras are present they will soon be seen hanging out into the water (Figure 24). The aquarium or jar should be kept out of direct sunlight, since hydras dislike strong light. If you want to keep the hydras indefinitely, plant a few sprays of Nitella, Elodea, Myriophyllum (Figure 25), or Vallisneria (Figure 26) in the aquarium to provide oxygen. The water should be maintained at a temperature of 20° C. or 68° F.

33

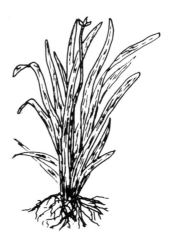

Figure 26
VALLISNERIA, EELGRASS

Hydras look like bits of coarse thread frayed out at one end. Look closely at the frayed ends and you will observe that they move or wave about. These frayed ends are the tentacles with which the hydra captures its food (Figure 21). The thread itself is the body, which is quite elastic, and as you watch the animal you will see that it can contract and expand at will (Figure 24). So, too, can the tentacles. These tentacles are provided with stinging cells, or capsules, and poison sacs arranged in batteries. Stinging cells occur on almost all parts of the hydra's body. There are four kinds of stinging cells, but basically they all discharge a threadlike structure that either penetrates or entangles a prospective prey. At one time it was believed that these stinging cells, called nematocysts, were triggered to explode by touch or a mechanical stimulus, but it has since been shown that they are exploded by a chemical stimulus. Place several hydras in a small dish of water and add a little acetic acid. As the acid diffuses through the water you can observe the discharge of the nematocysts. Hydras also respond to mechanical stimuli such as shocks. Tap the aquarium or agitate the surface of the water and you will note that they will immediately contract to the size of a pinhead (Figure 24). Once the disturbance has been removed they will gradually expand to their original condition.

Hydras feed on small crustaceans and worms, and these animals should also be collected. Perhaps they are already present in the water. Watching the hydras feed is a matter of patience. Although they are gluttonous feeders, they will not always react to food when presented to them. Even should an organism upon which the hydras normally feed come in contact with the tentacles this collision is not enough to cause the food-taking reaction, because the hydras will eat only after a certain interval of time has elapsed after their last meal.

As you watch your hydras you will observe that they hang from the plant stems or leaves (Figure 23) or even from the sides of the aquarium, stretching their bodies and tentacles into tenuous slenderness, circling slowly around within a radius of an inch or more. Should a hydra be ready for a meal, the moment the prey comes in contact with a tentacle the latter will immediately go into action and seize the prey (Figure 21). At the same time the other tentacles will come to the aid of the first and by collective teamwork will convey the prey to the mouth. A hydra swallows its food into a capacious central cavity, or stomach, and here the food is digested, the useless parts being cast out through the mouth, there being no special organ for this purpose. Hydras have practically insatiable appetites and will eat until their bodies become distended (Figure 27). You can even see the food being digested through their transparent sides, although you may need a hand lens to do so. In addition to small crustaceans and worms hydras feed on small insects and clams. They have even been observed eating small tadpoles and small fishes. So you should have no difficulty finding food for them. Should you, however, collect hydras in the winter, when their normal prey is scarce, you can feed them small bits of raw meat extended to them slowly with a forceps.

Figure 27
HYDRA AFTER HAVING GORGED ITSELF

Hydras reproduce both sexually by producing eggs and sperms, and asexually, by a process called budding (Figure 21). The two kinds of reproduction usually occur at different seasons. You can watch the process of budding in your aquarium. In this process a slight bulge appears on the body of the hydra. This bud pushes out rapidly as a projection that soon develops a circlet of blunt tentacles about the outer end. When full grown, the bud, which is now an individual hydra, detaches itself and lives a separate existence. The time required for a new hydra to form in this way is about two days under favorable conditions.

These interesting little freshwater animals

Figure 28
HYDRA MOVING IN A SERIES
OF LOOPING MOVEMENTS

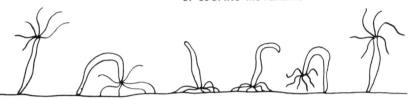

Figure 29
HYDRA MOVING IN A SERIES
OF CARTWHEELS

can move about by several methods; one, by gliding over the surface, to which they are attached, by means of their basal disk; a second, by a series of looping movements. By bending over, attaching their tentacles to the surface, then sliding the basal disk up close to the tentacles, and when in this position releasing the tentacles and assuming an upright position, they can move from place to place (Figure 28). A third method is by turning a series of somersaults or cartwheels. They release the basal disk from its point of attachment and swing it completely over, attaching

37

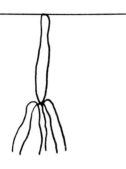

Figure 30
HYDRA HANGING FROM
SURFACE OF WATER

it to a new position, such end-over-end movements being repeated again and again (Figure 29). They also travel by a fourth method, which is seldom observed but which you may see. In this instance they move in an upside-down position, using their tentacles as legs. Sometimes you may see a hydra rise to the surface of the water and hang there for a while (Figure 30). To assist the animal to do so, a gas bubble forms at the basal disk.

ADVENTURE 6

We Encounter the Springtails

Figure 31
SPRINGTAIL

IN LITTLE BAYS of quiet water, formed by indentations of the shoreline, the surface of the water may often be covered with what appears to be a deposit of soot. On closer examination the "soot" turns out to be small black insects that have congregated on the surface. Create a slight disturbance and they all go into the air like flying spray. Look closely as they alight on the water and you will observe that they do so without making more than a dent on the surface film.

These insects are known as springtails (Figure 31). They are dull bluish black in color and very small, measuring only one-fifth to one-fourth of an inch in length, but in spite of their small size we can clearly see the body segments through a hand lens. They are most

38

grotesque and curious-looking creatures and, unlike most insects, lack wings. For this reason they were once believed to be degenerate descendants of winged creatures, but the present view is that they are primitive insects. Another point of interest is that the adults are exactly like the young; there are no stages of development, so typical of insects.

Examine a springtail closely and you will find it covered with fine hairs. These hairs hold a blanket of air, hence the body surface is difficult to wet. You will observe that it has six legs, but in spite of having six orthodox walking legs the insect has a unique locomotor apparatus on the hind end of its body. Look on the fourth abdominal segment, where you will find a forked tailpiece. The springtail can fold it beneath its body and lock it into two small appendages on the underside of the third abdominal segment. By releasing the tailpiece, which is springlike in its action, the insect is propelled into the air.

Springtails may be kept in a dish of water that should be covered with a piece of glass or other material, although they must have access to air. They can be fed microscopic algae, which can be collected from any pond or pool. For those of you who live near the seashore there is a marine species. It may be found walking on the surface film of tide pools between tidemarks or crawling on algae or under stones.

ADVENTURE 7

We Examine the Bottom Mud of Trashy Pools

Figure 32
ASELLUS, WATER ISOPOD

IN TRASHY POOLS where conditions appear unfavorable for any kind of life, small, broad-backed, flattened, grayish-brown creatures may usually be found crawling sluggishly about on the bottom mud or litter of decayed leaves.

These animals are known as water isopods and are commonly represented by Asellus (Figure 32). They have seven pairs of long legs and a hairy body that is invariably covered with silt. Two pairs of legs are adapted for grasping, the remaining pairs for walking. They feed on decaying plants and whatever dead animals may be present.

Isopods are of interest because they have a long breeding period and produce a brood of young every five or six weeks, and as they do well in captivity some interesting observations may be made of their breeding habits. The time to collect them is in February or early March, when their main breeding period begins. They can be kept in an aquarium or battery jar containing a quarter-inch layer of mud from the pool. A fairly large amount of

40

waterlogged bits of twigs, leaves, and other litter should also be place in the aquarium, which should be covered with a loose-fitting glass plate to keep out dust. It is advisable to use water from the pool, but tap water can be used if it has stood for a while. The aquarium should be filled to a depth of about an inch and kept in a cool place.

The female may be distinguished from the male by the brood pouch. An adult female produces about sixty eggs at a time and carries them in the brood pouch during their incubation.

They continue to breed throughout the summer and you will note that the females seem to be always carrying a brood pouch full of eggs or of young ones. Keep a record of the number of young isopods produced and the number of matings. Since green plants are absent, it is apparent that the isopods are not balanced against plants but against the atmosphere.

WE ARE often surprised at what we find when we go poking about in out-of-the-way places. If, for instance, we overturned the stones in the shallow riffles of a rapidly flowing stream we would likely uncover the hellgramite (Fig-

ADVENTURE 8

We Explore Shallow Riffles

ure 33), also known as the hell-diver, hell-devil, conniption bug, water grampus, flip-flap, snake doctor, dragon, or goggle goy.

Names usually do not mean much, but they can be descriptive, as in the present instance, for the hellgramite is a forbidding-looking creature. Seeing it for the first time, we would be loath to pick it up. Were we to do so we would probably drop it immediately. Upon being touched or irritated in any way, the hellgramite arches its body, stretches its jaws savagely, and presents a terrifying appearance. But it is harmless enough except to naiads of mayflies and stone-flies, upon which it feeds.

The hellgramite is a flattened, sprawling creature with large jaws, hairy legs, and a tough, thick skin. It may be dark brown, slate gray, or greenish black in color and when full grown measures two or three inches in length. There is a tuft of white hairlike gills at the base of each of the lateral appendages on the first seven abdominal segments, and there is also a pair of stout, fleshy prolegs, each armed with a pair of grappling hooks, at the end of the abdomen. The animal shuns light and is seldom seen unless stones are overturned or pulled from the riffles when it clings to the surface or hitches itself rapidly backward by its posterior grappling hooks.

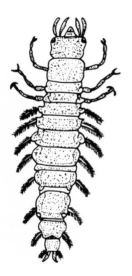

Figure 33
HELLGRAMITE

42

The hellgramite is the larval stage of an insect generally known as the dobsonfly; it takes two to three years to mature. The adult is a large winged insect with a cinnamon brown body and grayish-white spotted wings that measure four or five inches from tip to tip when fully expanded. The adult dobsonfly is rather short-lived, and though it has strong jaws it takes no food as far as we know. Unlike the larva, the adult dobson is often attracted to light, especially at night. Sometimes we find several dobsons flying high about street lights.

Hellgramites are difficult to keep in an aquarium for any length of time, as they live in rapidly flowing streams and it is difficult to simulate their natural environment without elaborate equipment. However, if you wish to observe a hellgramite transform into an adult dobson it can be done quite easily. Arrange an aquarium with water at one end and soil at the other for the hellgramite migrates to land when ready to pupate. Then look for a nearly full-grown hellgramite about to transform. Place it in the aquarium and keep it under observation. Pupation usually takes place in May and June.

ADVENTURE 9

*We Investigate Jet
Propulsion*

IN THIS SPACE AGE of ours we speak of rockets, rocket ships, and jet airplanes and regard them as quite an achievement. Certain insects discovered or developed the principle we employ in propelling these forms of aircraft and spacecraft aeons ago, although they use water instead of hot burning gases. The principle involved is Newton's third law of motion: that for every action there is an equal and opposite reaction.

If this statement doesn't mean much to you, perhaps an example will make it clearer. Probably you have had the experience of getting out of a boat and stepping upon the shore or wharf and have noticed that as you stepped forward the boat was pushed backward. In other words you pushed the boat backward but at the same time the boat pushed you forward. Another example of this law can be illustrated by means of a roller skate. Step on a roller skate with one foot and take a step forward and you will observe that the skate moves backward in the opposite direction. The same principle can also be shown with a toy balloon. Blow one up, pinch the neck, and then release it. The balloon will move forward as the jet of air escapes and pushes against the outside air.

Now you are doubtless familiar with the dragonflies, often called the devil's darning needles. They occur in the vicinity of ponds, streams, and lakes, where they may be seen flying through the air like arrows. The young, known as naiads, live in the water until they are full grown and are ready to transform, when they climb up on land. They may be found throughout the year crawling about the bottom mud looking for prey during the warmer months of the year, buried in the mud in winter.

It is these naiads that make use of jet propulsions as a means of getting through the water. To observe how they do so, we need only collect a few and place them in a dishpan or similar container. It is much easier to collect them during the summer, when all you need do is drag a scoop or pan along the bottom among the vegetation. In winter we have to dredge up some of the bottom mud and then go over it carefully for any naiads buried in it.

To understand how they can propel themselves through the water we must first learn how they breathe beneath the surface. Examine a naiad carefully and you will note the absence of any visible or external breathing organ. The reason is that the gills, with which they extract the oxygen from the water, are located internally. Known as rectal tracheal gills, they are located in a special chamber

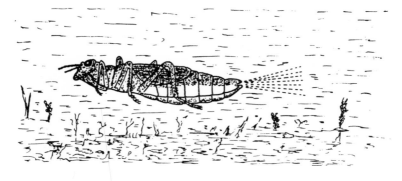

Figure 34
DRAGONFLY NAIAD PROPELLED
THROUGH WATER BY
JET PROPULSION

in the rear of the alimentary canal (the rectum) and consist of an elaborate lacework of air tubes formed by an infolding of the rectal walls. Water is drawn in and out of this gill chamber through an anal orifice guarded by elaborate strainers or, more specifically, by five pointed spines. At times the water is forcibly expelled by the contraction of the abdominal muscles and when this occurs the insect is shot through the water (Figure 34). The breathing apparatus of the dragonfly naiad thus serves a double function: as an organ of respiration and as one of locomotion.

Dragonfly naiads can be kept in an aquarium for long periods, if you wish to observe and study them at length, but since they are carnivorous they must be given a constant supply of small live water insects, worms, and similar items.

46

COUNTLESS EXAMPLES of camouflage may be found among animals, although in many instances some other word or expression is used because it may be somewhat more definitive. In its broadest sense camouflage means to blend with the surroundings for the purpose of concealment, but where an animal secures such concealment because its general form resembles some object of its surroundings or background we call it protective resemblance.

An excellent example of protective resemblance is the water scorpion, Ranatra (Figure 35), which is rather a misnomer, for the animal is not a scorpion but an insect. It may be found among dead leaves and trash along the shoreline of a pond or stream, but it looks so much like a brown, waterlogged stick that it is difficult to distinguish from the twigs lying on the bottom until it starts to walk about. Even then it appears so much like a twig being carried by the water that it is often overlooked.

Although they have a forbidding appearance, water scorpions may safely be picked up with the fingers. What appears to be a long sting is actually a breathing tube that they extend above the surface of the water. They are usually found on the bottom along the shoreline in shallow water but may frequently be seen clinging to the stems of rushes and

We See a Stick That Moves

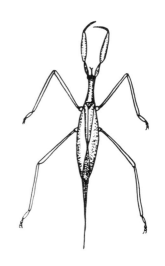

Figure 35
RANATRA, WATER SCORPION

47

sedges in deeper water, with the respiratory tube piercing the surface film, and upon floating leaves and stalks of cattails. The breathing apparatus, which resembles the sting of the scorpion, consists of two long filaments that form a tube for conducting the air to two spiracles situated at the caudal end of the abdomen.

Examine the breathing tube with a hand lens and observe how the front legs are fitted for grasping prey. The water scorpion is a rapacious creature, preying on pond-dwelling mayflies and tender young damselflies, whose body juices it sucks by means of its short but powerful beak.

When you remove a water scorpion from the water, listen carefully for a faint squeak that it makes by rubbing a roughened patch on the outside of each front leg against a rasp on the inner margin of each shoulder of the prothorax. Water scorpions may be kept in an aquarium or in a light-colored, shallow enameled pan if you want to observe their habits. They are normally sluggish creatures in their native habitat, remaining motionless for hours on the muddy leaf-covered bottom, so don't expect too much activity on their part. They may be fed any kind of living insect and pieces of raw meat. Since they eat the latter they can be kept in captivity during

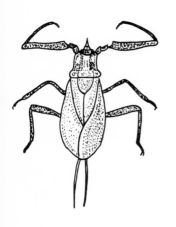

Figure 36
NEPA, WATER SCORPION

48

the winter and may be collected by scooping or raking some of the mud and trash out of the water.

There is another species of water scorpion, Nepa (Figure 36), which is quite different in appearance, being oval, flat, and thin. Nepa looks even more dead and lifeless than its cousin, but its apparent lifelessness is merely a ruse to lure mayfly naiads, snails, or crustaceans within reach of its front legs. Water scorpions of both species do not lose their appetites easily, as you will discover should you place other insects in with them.

The eggs of water scorpions are unusual, since they are furnished with a crown of filaments, seven in Nepa and two in Ranatra (Figure 37). As the eggs are inserted into the decayed tissues of plants, leaving the filaments exposed, the latter wave about in the water currents.

Figure 37
EGG OF WATER SCORPION, RANATRA

ADVENTURE 11

We Play Nursemaid

IN LATE APRIL or early May (the time may vary slightly in different parts of the country) countless toads may be seen in ponds or spring pools mating and laying their eggs. To watch a toad develop from a tiny embryonic speck in the egg to an adult toad, passing through a amphibious life as a tadpole in the process, is a most interesting and rewarding experience and one we can all have with a minimum of effort and equipment.

The equipment consists of an enameled pan (a good size is one and a half feet in diameter and about eight inches deep), a pail, a metal dipper or small pan, and several jars such as Mason jars. With these supplies go to the nearest pond or pool where toads are laying their eggs and remove some of the small, algae-covered stones lying on the bottom or along the edge, lifting them gently so as not to disturb the algae growing on them. Place the stones on the bottom of the pan, building up one side higher than the other so the depth of the water will vary, being shallower on one side than the other and leaving a few stones projecting above the water. Then add some of the mud and leaves from the pond bottom. If there are any plants growing in the pond, transplant a few of them among the stones.

Except for filling it with water the pan aquarium is now ready to receive the eggs. Toad eggs are laid in long, curling tubes of jelly containing a single row of black eggs (Figure 38). As the eggs lack a shell and should be handled gently, exercise the utmost care in removing them from the water, using a metal dipper or small pan. Place the eggs in

Figure 38
TOAD EGGS

the Mason jars and then fill the pail with pond water.

Returning home, place the pan aquarium away from all artificial heat and where it will receive direct sunshine for a part of the day through an open window, but do not let the water get too warm. Next fill the pan aquarium nearly to the brim with the pond water from the pail, pouring the water in gently at one side so as not to disarrange the plants. When the mud has settled, introduce the eggs. As the aquarium can accommodate only a few tadpoles, do not place too many eggs in it. The tubes of jelly contain far more eggs than can be used, so cut off a length containing about a dozen. Distribute the remaining eggs among several bowls or glass dishes filled with pond water, as a reserve supply should anything happen to the eggs in the aquarium and they fail to hatch. To be successful raising tadpoles, remember not to overcrowd or overheat them. More water animals die from these two causes than from any other.

Once the eggs are in the aquarium, keep a close watch on them, and should any turn white remove them immediately and replace them with eggs from the reserve supply or they will pollute the water. The reason they turn white is that they are either dead or infested with fungi; healthy eggs soon turn dark.

Figure 39
**EGGS SHOW HEAD AND TAIL
ENDS OF TADPOLES**

Meanwhile you can observe changes taking place within the eggs and before long you will find that they are no longer eggs but developing tadpoles in which a head and tail (Figure 39) can be distinguished. Within three or four days tadpoles begin to emerge from the eggs. Look closely for two small suckers where the mouth should be (Figure 40). These suckers secrete a sticky substance that the young tadpoles use to attach themselves to weeds, grasses, and algae or to the sides of the aquarium. At first tadpoles do not require feeding but rely essentially on the stored nourishment in their tails.

In about two days from the time of hatching, the head, body, and tail may be seen more clearly. Look at a tadpole from above or from below and note the conspicuous fingerlike extensions in the neck region. These extensions are gills. Although they have been present for forty-eight hours or more, they were so small and delicate they were not easily seen. For the first few days tadpoles are not active and show only a vigorous wiggling of

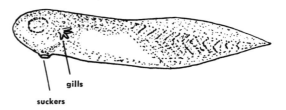

gills

suckers

Figure 40
YOUNG TADPOLE

the tail when disturbed but gradually they become more active and begin to make short circuitous trips.

When about a week old the head has become somewhat larger and the gills less conspicuous. They are now farther back on the neck. The reason for this apparent dislocation is that a membrane has begun to grow backward from the anterior part of the head. This membrane eventually covers the gills and neck region, making the tadpoles look as if they consisted of a large head and tail but no body.

About ten days after hatching the tadpoles appear like tiny black coals with a continually wiggling tail and a small round mouth that seems to be constantly searching for food. The mouth is now open and functional and is provided with horny jaws for scraping off the tissues of plant stems and leaves.

When the tadpoles are from four to six weeks old and approaching their full development, they measure about one inch long, the tail taking up about three-fifths of the entire length. The soft skin is nearly black, but with a lens a faint stippling of gold can be detected. The eyes are small, the pupil being round and black and surrounded by an iridescent iris, and two nostrils appear as small white openings.

The tadpoles now breathe by means of internal gills. The water enters through the nostrils and mouth, which is continually opening and closing, and passes through openings in the side wall of the throat, then over the gills, to emerge from a funnel-shaped opening at the left side.

The first sign that the tadpoles are beginning to change into toads is the appearance of the hind legs (Figure 41). At first they are mere rounded buds, but soon joints and toes develop and before long the legs are fully formed. The tadpoles now use the legs as well as the tail in swimming.

In two weeks or less after the appearance of the hind legs the front ones suddenly appear (Figure 42), and they are fully formed. This may seem surprising, yet they have been developing at the same time as the hind ones but have been hidden beneath the gill membrane. The left one is extended through the breathing pore, the right one breaks directly

Figure 41
TADPOLE WITH HIND LEGS
BEGINNING TO SHOW

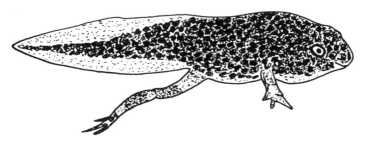

through the skin. Other changes have also occurred. The small mouth has been replaced by a large one with an opening that now extends far back beneath the eyes, which have increased in size and have become elevated so that they appear like the eyes of adult toads. The tail has become shorter and will continue to become shorter, being absorbed from within until it has become a mere stub, eventually to disappear.

The tadpoles have at last become perfect toads, but they are small and their brown skin is smooth, showing none of the warts we associate with toads (Figure 43). Size and a warty skin will come, however, as they gradually mature, in two to three years. Remarkable as the external changes may be, more so are the internal changes that have taken place. Gills have been superseded by lungs with an attendant shift in circulation, and the diges-

55

Figure 43
TOADLET

tive system of the insect-eating toad is quite
different from that of the plant-eating tadpole.

Should you undertake to play nursemaid
to developing tadpoles, it is advisable to add
each week a little more mud from the pond
and perhaps an algae-covered stone or two.
Also add water from time to time to replace
that which evaporates, but use water from the
pond and not tap water. If you can obtain a
tulip leaf, remove the "skin" from one side to
expose the pulp, and give some of this pulp to
your tadpoles every day or two. Bits of hard-
boiled egg may also be given from time to
time but remove any not eaten or the water
will turn foul. If you follow these simple
directions you should have no trouble raising
tadpoles. By July they should have become
small toads and ready to leave the water.
Transfer them to a terrarium where you can
watch them grow and mature into full-fledged
adult toads.

WE GENERALLY associate clams and mussels with the seashore. Some of us have dug for clams in the wet sand at low tide, and most of us who have visited the seacoast have found countless mussels in tide pools among the rocks. But clams and mussels are also found in freshwaters, where they make up a very large part of pond and stream populations.

Mussels and clams belong to a group of animals known as the mollusks, a group that includes the snails, oysters, slugs, and the lesser known chitons, squids, and octopi. All these animals have soft, unsegmented bodies and hard shells, although in the squid and octopus the shell is concealed in a mantle of flesh.

All our freshwater mussels and clams are bivalves, that is, each has a shell with two valves, or shell parts, and a fleshy, burrowing, hatchet-shaped foot, hence they are known as the Pelecypoda, or hatchet-footed. They use the foot to plough their way through the bottom mud of ponds and streams (Figure 44), but they usually lie relaxed on the bottom, with the valves slightly apart and the foot projected out between them, when they look very much as if they had their tongues out. Perhaps you have heard the expression that mussels "lie on the bottom with their tongues out."

We Become Acquainted with Some Clams and Mussels

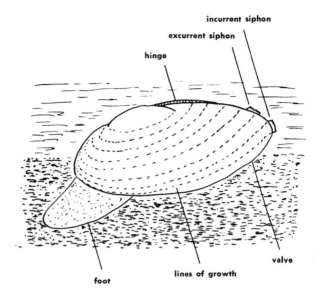

incurrent siphon

excurrent siphon

hinge

valve

lines of growth

foot

Figure 44
FRESHWATER MUSSEL

Examine a mussel closely (Figure 44) and locate at the rear, or posterior, end of the body, the narrower part of the valve, the two tubelike siphons. Water enters through the lower, incurrent siphon, carrying with it food and oxygen. By means of moving microscopic cilia, borne upon the mantle and body surfaces, the water is made to pass over the gills toward the mouth and then outward through the upper, excurrent siphon, picking up waste materials on its way out. Mussels and clams do not have heads, but the

58

mouth is located at the anterior end, which is the wider part of the valve.

The valves are held together along the dorsal, or top, margin by a springlike hinge (Figure 44), an exceedingly tough, leathery substance and in many instances shut by a system of interlocking teeth which project from the hinge. The two valves open automatically when not held or pulled together by two large adductor muscles whose opposite ends are attached to opposing shells. When the two valves are closed there is a resultant strain on the adductor muscle in overcoming the elasticity of the hinge, and when this strain is removed or when the mussel relaxes the adductors, the valves open. Thus it is that when a mussel dies the valves gape apart because the adductors no longer function.

The valves are formed by the hardened secretions of certain cells in the mantle, a fleshy outgrowth of the outer body wall. Look closely at the outer surface of one of the valves and observe a number of lines or rings. They are lines of growth (Figure 44) and like the rings of a tree show the amount of growth between successive periods of activity and inactivity in shell formation. Additions or new growth are built on at the edge of the valve and here the valve is newest and thinnest. In the larger mussels the valve has three layers: an outer dark, horny layer, the periostracum; a thick middle, or prismatic, layer of lime; and an inner nacreous, or pearly, layer.

In small mussels both male and female reproductive organs occur in the same individual, but in the large species eggs are produced by one individual and sperms by another. Eggs pass from the ovary into the mantle cavity, the space between the mantle and the body, and then into the gills of the female. Each gill is a flattened sac partitioned into water tubes, and the eggs are carried into the open tops by currents of water. These currents of water, which have entered through the incurrent siphon, also carry the sperms, which have been discharged into the open water by a male. Fertilization of the eggs takes place in the gills, which become the female's brood pouch, each water tube being filled with fertilized eggs like peas in a pod. Here the developing embryos remain until they have become free-swimming young or larval mussels (glochidia) with their first juvenile shells.

The number of glochidia produced varies according to the species—there may be from seventy-five thousand to three million of them. Few, however, ever live to become full grown mussels. The reason is that they must become attached to fishes to survive.

In the young mussels, or glochidia (Figure 45), the valves are opened and shut intermittently by the single adductor muscle. Place a few glochidia on a piece of glass and look at them with a hand lens. You should be able to see their convulsive snapping. To obtain the glochidia, collect a number of mussels, then wait until they have relaxed and the valves open. Insert a plug between them to keep them open. Select one of the mussels and push a pipette through the thin wall of the brood pouch and slowly withdraw it. If you have a gravid female, the glochidia will come out with the pipette. If you are unsuccessful with the first mussel, try another and again another until you have obtained the glochidia. There is no well-defined difference in the shells of the two sexes, so you will have to get your glochidia by the trial-and-error method.

The persistent snapping is a provision of nature to ensure the survival of the glochidia once they have left the brood pouch. At the very moment they come in contact with a fish they clamp their shells into whatever part of the fish they touch. The skin of the fish then grows over them and, thus protected and nourished by the body fluids of the fish, they live a parasitic existence for several weeks

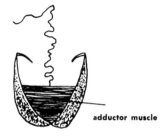

adductor muscle

Figure 45
GLOCHIDIUM

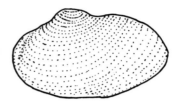

Figure 46
ANODONTA, PAPER-SHELL CLAM

or until they have become mature. Strangely enough the glochidia of a given species of mussel will attach themselves only to a certain species of fish. Should they become attached to the wrong species, so sensitive are they to their chemical environment and to differences in body fluids that they will soon drop off.

One of the best species of mussels from which to collect a few glochidia for observation is the paper-shell, *Anodonta cataracta* (Figure 46), a common species occurring in muddy streams and ponds. The greenish or brown valves are thin, generally smooth and shining, and are often winged posteriorly.

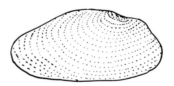

Figure 47
ELLIPTIO, PEARLY MUSSEL

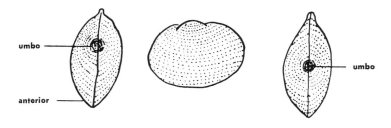

Figure 48
SPHAERIUM, FINGERNAIL CLAM

The paper-shell mussel breeds in late summer, but the glochidia are not discharged until the following spring. Hence gravid females can be found in shallow waters through the winter. Since there is no well defined difference in the shells of the two sexes, it is advisable to collect enough to ensure obtaining a few females.

Another common species is the pearly mussel, *Elliptio complanatus* (Figure 47), found on gravelly shores between rocks or on muddy bottoms. The valves are thick and oval or elongate with smooth or slightly corrugated surfaces. The breeding season extends from April to May, and the glochidia are freed into the water from August through September, so this will permit you to obtain glochidia during the summer.

There are a number of other freshwater mollusks with which you might like to be-

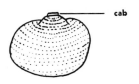

cab

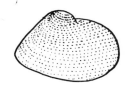

Figure 49
MUSCULIUM, FINGERNAIL CLAM

Figure 50
PISIDIUM, PILL CLAM

come acquainted, such as the fingernail clams and pill clams. Fingernail clams, of the genus Sphaerium (Figure 48), are small, about half an inch in length. The valves are thin, ovoid or oval, and usually white or yellowish with a centrally placed umbo, the swollen part of the valves and the first part to develop. They occur in lakes, rivers, ponds, pools, and small streams, where they live on the bottom of sand, mud, or clay; sometimes they creep upon the plants.

Fingernail clams of the genus Musculium resemble those of Sphaerium except for a little cap on the umbo (Figure 49). They live in the same haunts. The pill clams, Pisidium, are minute, measuring one-eighth to three-eighths of an inch in length. The valves are round or oval, greenish or yellowish, with the umbo placed a little back of the middle (Figure 50). They live in varied habitats and not only burrow in the mud but climb upon plants.

64

DURING the months of April and May look into a roadside ditch partially filled with water and you may see what appears to be horsehairs twisting and wiggling about.

These wiggling "horsehairs" are popularly known as horsehair snakes. They are neither horsehairs nor snakes but worms, known as hairworms (Figure 51). They occur not only in roadside ditches but in ponds, brooks, and springs, where they lie on the bottom either singly or in groups. When in groups they are twisted together and look like a snarl of twine, loose-coiled wire, or matted roots. They measure a foot or two long and their bodies are entirely covered with a thin layer of horny brown chitin. This material gives them a certain stiffness so when they slowly coil and uncoil they look like wire come to life. The body tapers to a point at the anterior end, but at the opposite end it is split into two or three parts, according to the sex and species (Figure 52).

The worms appear in the spring, probably having spent the winter in the mud, and soon after lay their eggs in the water. They are minute, pure white, and strung like beads along translucent threads that are suspended from submerged water plants. Soon after the eggs are laid the adults die. The eggs hatch into small, almost microscopic young that

We Look into a Roadside Ditch

Figure 51
HAIR WORM

Figure 52
BILOBED TAIL OF MALE (a)
TRILOBED TAIL OF FEMALE (b)

swim about in the water. Some of them drop to the bottom, others wiggle on to the wet soil of the shore or upon plants growing there. Most of the young worms die, since they can survive only if they manage to penetrate a mayfly naiad or some other aquatic insect, into which they bore by means of bristles on the head, or if they are ingested by a grasshopper, cricket, or beetle that ventures near the water's edge. Once within the host they grow until they reach maturity.

The worms that mature within an aquatic insect have only to leave their host to get into the water, where they become sexually mature, but those that have become full grown within a terrestrial insect, such as a grasshopper or cricket, must reach the water to survive. Most of these latter worms perish, for grasshoppers or crickets are not generally found along the water's edge or if they get near the water may not do so at the right time. However, should infested grasshoppers or crickets get to the water at the right time, the worms burrow their way out and drop into the water. How they know when the host has reached water is not known, but probably they are influenced by moisture.

In late summer you might collect a few grasshoppers or crickets occurring in the vicinity of a pond or brook and place them in a dish of water. Some worms may issue from them.

IN PONDS and brooks we often find a rock or log covered with a mosslike growth that we assume is a clump of small plants but that on closer inspection we discover is a colony of animals.

These animals are popularly known as moss animals, technically the Bryozoa, which means moss animals. They occur in all kinds of freshwater—ponds, stagnant pools, and rushing streams—where they live in sessile, plantlike colonies of hundreds or thousands of individuals on lily pads, submerged twigs, the undersides of flattened stones that they cover with delicate traceries, and on logs and boards, where they form a vinelike growth. In some species the individual animals (zooids) live in brown tubes of lime; in others in a soft, transparent matrix of jelly. The bryozoans are an interesting group of animals, and one should become better acquainted with them.

As the zooids are so small that they can be seen only with a hand lens or a microscope, it is best to remove a colony from the water and transfer it to an aquarium or a dish of

We Visit an Animal Garden

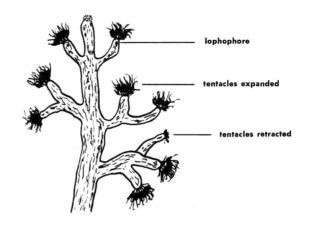

lophophore

tentacles expanded

tentacles retracted

Figure 53
PLUMATELLA, A BRYOZOAN

water. The animals are sensitive to any kind of disturbance and will retreat within their tubes or jelly when molested, but if left undisturbed for a few minutes they will slowly emerge and unfold a beautiful crown of tentacles like the blossoming of a delicate flower. Examine one of the tentacles and you will observe that each has a horseshoe-shaped ridge called the lophophore (Figure 53). This is the head "region" and bears the tentacles, which are provided with cilia. The cilia direct currents of water carrying food particles toward the mouth, located in the midst of the tentacles. When undisturbed the bryozoans constantly rotate their headlike lophophores, but jar the dish or aquarium ever so slightly and they quickly disappear from view.

The food canal of the bryozoans is a U-shaped tube that leads downward from the mouth and then turns sharply upward, with the anus just inside or just outside the circle of tentacles (Figure 54). The body is very flexible below the tentacles and is provided with muscles by which the animals pull themselves into their limy tubes or withdraw into their protecting caps of jelly. Once you have seen how quickly they can disappear, you will realize how effectively these animals can protect themselves from enemies.

The growth of a colony is by budding, which we described in Adventure 5. New colonies, however, are started by individuals in the spring either from sex cells or from winter buds called statoblasts. The statoblasts are resistant to drought and cold and are designed to carry the animals over the winter. They are groups of cells that form within the body of an individual bryozoan and are set free in the water after the animal has died and its outer covering has disintegrated. Some statoblasts are enclosed in tough cushions that buoy them up like preservers (Figure 55); others are provided with hooks that anchor them to various objects (Figure 56). Many are washed up on the shores of ponds

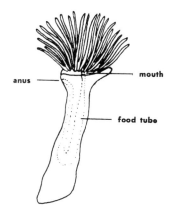

Figure 54
INDIVIDUAL ZOOID

Figure 55
STATOBLAST OF PLUMATELLA

69

Figure 56
STATOBLAST OF PECTINATELLA

and lakes, where they may be found in long dark ribbons on the sand; others float in brown films on the water surface. Not a few of those that have hooks are carried about by animals and especially by water birds that distribute them far and wide.

Although statoblasts germinate in abundance in the spring, this is not the only time when they can do so. The statoblasts of some species germinate regularly in the summer. Most of them, however, are formed in late summer and autumn, when the bryozoans begin to die, and remain in the water throughout the winter. During the fall and early winter they can be found adhering to stones and water plants and may be scraped or lifted off with a knife. It may be of interest to collect a few and germinate them. Fill a dish with two or three inches of water, preferably pond water, which should be clean and cool (about 68° F.), and place it in moderate light. Transfer the statoblasts to clean microscope slides or to pieces of broken glass rinsed with pure water, and put the slides in the dish. Allow them to remain undisturbed except for adding a little fresh water poured in gently at the side of the dish. They will germinate in a week or less if all goes well.

A few of the more familiar bryozoans are Paludicella, Plumatella, Fredericella, Pec-

tinatella, and Cristatella, the last-mentioned
not as common as the others. Colonies of
Paludicella (Figure 57) are composed of delicate, jointed branching, club-shaped recum-
bent or partly erect tubes, placed end to end
and separated from one another by partitions,
that creep over stones and sticks. Plumatella
colonies (Figure 53) consist of cylindrical
tubes that form a vinelike growth or massive
clumps and occur in a variety of places.
Sometimes they are so abundant on sluice-
ways and weirs of reservoirs that they can be
removed with shovels. Fredericella (Figure
58) forms branching colonies that are partly

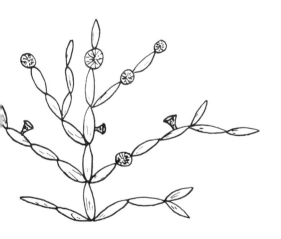

Figure 57
PALUDICELLA

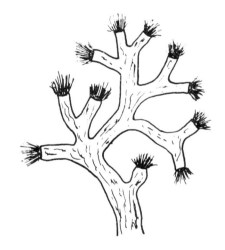

Figure 58
FREDERICELLA

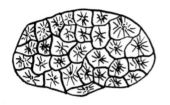

Figure 59
PECTINATELLA

creeping and partly erect with antler-like branches, or dense clumps on the undersides of sticks and stones usually in dark places. Pectinatella (Figure 59) consists of many associated colonies in rosette groups clustered on the surface of large masses of jelly that adhere to sticks and stones or hang from twigs and water plants. Colonies of Cristatella (Figure 60) are elongate or oval, rug-like gelatinous masses and measure from one to two inches long. They occur most frequently on the undersides of leaves, especially lily pads, and are remarkable because they are capable of a slow creeping movement; the entire colony acts as a unit. To view a colony of bryozoans as they wave their tentacles about is to peer into a miniature garden of delicate transparent flowers. A more beautiful sight is difficult to find with a hand lens.

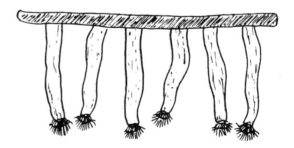

Figure 60
CRISTATELLA

SOMETIMES animals are adapted to live in an environment in which it would appear impossible for them to exist. Consider the small, seemingly delicate blackflies that live among the rocks of a waterfall or in the rapids of a rushing stream.

More accurately it is the larvae that find conditions most congenial in rushing waters, where we would expect them to be carried downstream or hurled against the rocks. Locate a waterfall or a rapids and see how they manage to survive. From May to midsummer is a good time to find them. Look for what appears to be a swaying mass of greenish "black moss" on a rock (Figure 61), stick, or leaf. The "black moss" is made up of thousands of larvae, and by scooping up a handful you can collect hundreds of them.

Figure 61
LARVAE OF BLACKFLY ON STONE IN RAPIDS

Figure 62
LARVA OF BLACKFLY

Examine one of the larvae (Figure 62) with a hand lens. At the hind end is a disklike sucker fringed with little hooks. It uses these hooks to cling to a rock, stick, or other support. At the opposite end just behind the head is a fleshy proleg that is also provided with a sucker. With these two suckers the insect is able to walk over the rocks, stones, or other surfaces in a sort of looping gait. What happens if the larva is dislodged by the rushing water, which happens frequently? It spins a silken thread from its salivary glands and attaches this to its resting place. Then with the aid of the hooks on the caudal sucker, which are nicely fitted to cling to the thread, the larva hangs on to its anchorage.

You can observe this if you place a white plate, which will provide a background for the dark-colored larvae, beneath the rock, stone, stick, leaf, or whatever object to which you find the larvae clinging. As you place the plate beneath the object, many of the insects, disturbed by your movements, will let go and drift a few inches away. There they remain stationary, and if you look closely you will find a number of threads visible on the white plate. Sometimes the threads become covered with small plant particles or other debris that makes them more distinct. The threads may extend in all directions from one rock to another or from one leaf to another and thus provide the insects with a labyrinth along which they can make their way to a new place of attachment or return to their old anchorage. The threads are not spun at the moment of being disturbed, but are old threads previously spun. However, these insects can spin new threads in an emergency. When disturbed, all the larvae do not let go; as a matter of fact, they are not easily frightened, and most of them remain in place attached by their suckers. By means of the silken threads the insects can travel downstream, swinging from rock to rock.

Examine a larva again. Note at the anterior, or head, end the two fan-shaped brushes. The insect uses these brushes to collect its food, which consists chiefly of algae and diatoms. Respiration is effected by three retractile blood gills on the dorsal side of the last abdominal segment.

When full grown, the larva spins a boot-shaped or basketlike cocoon (Figure 63) that it attaches to a rock or other object or to other cocoons. Frequently the cocoons are so numerous that they form golden-brown blankets on the rocks which are even more moss-like than those of the larvae. The pupa (Figure 64) breathes through tracheal gills. The respiratory filaments project from the top of

Figure 63
COCOON OF BLACKFLY

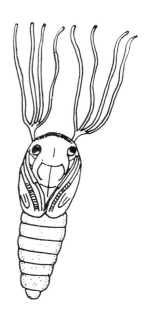

Figure 64
PUPA OF BLACKFLY

75

each cocoon and wave about in the water. When the adult flies emerge from the pupal skins, they rise to the surface of the water and take flight at once. Soon after they mate and lay their eggs. Should you visit a waterfall or rapids when the flies are laying their eggs, you can observe them darting in and out of the water. Since the flies bite, it is advisable to use some blackfly cream or a similar concoction on your hands and face and other exposed parts of your body.

ADVENTURE 16

We Observe an Unusual Event

FISHES, as a rule, do not build nests. Some of our native fishes, however, make a circular depression in the bottom sand or mud of a pond or stream as a repository for their eggs. The brook stickleback goes beyond such a crude structure and builds a nest that rivals some of those made by birds.

A remarkable example of piscine architecture, it is a delicate globular affair, about three-quarters of an inch in diameter, with a hole in one side, and made of fine fibers, plant stems, and algae filaments. In brooks and small streams the nest is difficult to detect against a background of leaves and plant stems and is discovered only by accident. Fortunately the stickleback does very well in an aquarium and with a little effort and care its mating and nest-building habits may be observed.

The brook stickleback is found in small streams and bogs, where it lives among the waterweeds. A small, slender, graceful fish, between two and three inches long (the male is somewhat smaller than the female) and pointed anteriorly like an arrow, it has a row of sharp, upstanding spines along its back. Four of the spines are free, the fifth one is attached to the dorsal fin. When seen among the waterweeds it is greenish, mottled with paler green, but when swimming or resting near the bottom it appears much darker. In spring during the breeding season the back of the male becomes almost black, lightening to dull yellow beneath; the female at this time is olive colored with brown blotches.

The stickleback does best in a large aquarium stocked with adequate plant life. In preparing the aquarium make sure that it is clean. Then place an inch or so of good garden soil, free from manure and plant remains, and cover this layer with an inch or so of clean washed sand. Next fill the aquarium, preferably with clean water from the stream where you expect to get your stickleback. Tap water may be used if it is allowed to stand for several days. When filling the aquarium pour the water in gently so as not to stir up the sand and soil. Although oxygenating plants may be obtained at any pet store where tropical fish are sold, it is best to get plants* from the same stream as the fish. When planting be sure that only the roots are covered; the crown or the juncture of roots and leaves should be just clear (Figure 65). Place the plants about an inch apart along the back and the two sides of the aquarium, leaving the front unobstructed for viewing purposes, and not too close to the glass sides so you can clean them without

* Especially such plants as Elodea or Vallisneria.

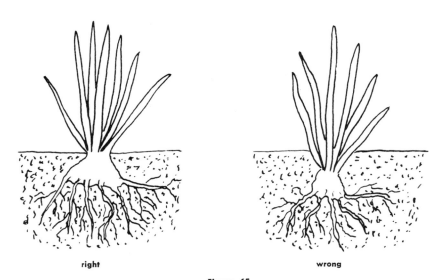

right   wrong

Figure 65
RIGHT AND WRONG WAYS OF
PLANTING AQUARIUM PLANTS

damage to the plants. Set larger plants at the rear and along the sides and the smaller plants in front of them.

With the plants in place cover the aquarium with a piece of glass to prevent evaporation of the water and to prevent dust and other foreign materials from settling on the surface. Then locate the aquarium in a good light, near a window. A diffused light with about two hours of direct sunlight is ideal. Two precautions should be observed. Do not place the aquarium near a radiator or too near a window during the winter months, as the water is likely to become chilled during the nighttime. As frequently happens, a green coating of algae may form on the glass side nearest the window and perhaps on the sides as well. Ordinarily this coating should not be removed, as it will serve the double purpose of diffusing the sunlight and of helping to aerate the water; however, if it forms on the front it should be removed or it will obstruct your view of the interior.

In order to obtain the maximum results the aquarium should stand unmolested for about a week before the fish are placed in it, to allow the plants to become well rooted and the water amply aerated. When all is in readiness the next step is to procure the fish. The best way to collect the sticklebacks is with a seine, which should be fine-meshed (about three-fourths of an inch) and supplied with lead weights, floats, and tie cords. The net should be about ten feet long and four feet deep, with a round, concave center trap that extends out in the rear. In collecting you will need an assistant. One of you should hold the upper tie cord of one end of the net and, dressed in rubber boots, walk slowly upstream, while the other walks along the bank holding the other end of the net. Maintain a slow, steady pace without any splashing. Of course you should make sure beforehand that the stream contains sticklebacks. If you do not care to use a seine you can use a dip net. (Figure 66). Even a minnow trap of the fun-

Figure 66
DIP NET

nel type may be useful. Before you set out to collect your sticklebacks, check the fishing laws, as a fishing license may be required to collect native fish of any kind.

As sticklebacks are pugnacious, greedy, and quarrelsome, only a mating pair should be kept in the aquarium. Do not keep other fish or even snails with them. Autumn is the best time to collect the sticklebacks. At this time of the year they are in good condition

80

and it is easier for them to become accustomed to the close confines of an aquarium. If the aquarium is well balanced, you should not have to change the water and only occasionally you might find it necessary to remove any debris that settles on the bottom. Sticklebacks thrive best on natural foods such as small crustaceans like Daphnia and Cyclops,* midge larvae,† and other small insects, but in captivity will take medium tropical-fish food, very small bits of ground raw

* See Adventures 35 and 42.
† See Adventure 29.

Figure 67
STICKLEBACK BUILDING
HIS NEST

beef, and thin earthworms in quarter-inch sections. Unless the main stems of some of the aquarium plants are large and strong, it is advisable to place a stout twig in the sand to which the male fish can anchor his nest.

When mating time arrives, the male stickleback first selects his nest site, then bites off pieces of plant stems and algae filaments which he fashions into a small sphere (Figure 67), using a cementlike substance from his kidneys to hold them together. He also uses this substance to line the inside walls and to give the nest rigidity and firmness, smoothing the walls by repeatedly pushing his head and body against them. The entire nest structure is attached to the submerged plant stems or a twig.

The nest completed, the male swims out to woo his mate. Courtship is a vigorous affair with considerable "dancing," pursuing, nipping, and butting. Finally, the female, through a mixture of coaxing and coercion, since both seem to be involved, accompanies the male to his nest and enters it. She remains within the nest for a while, laying her eggs, while the male remains outside on guard, swimming around and around it. After the eggs are laid the female emerges and swims away, whereupon the male enters the nest and fertilizes the eggs by discharging his sperm cells over them. Thereafter he remains on guard while the eggs are incubating and until they hatch. There is no reason for him to stand guard in the aquarium (in his natural habitat he must do so to ward off any intruders), but his instinctive behavior is so strong that he must follow the natural sequence of events that constitute the normal pattern of mating and nest building. The young sticklebacks are quite hardy and will thrive in the aquarium, but the adults should be removed two or three days after the young have emerged or they might become cannibalistic and devour their progeny.

MOST OF US have seen small insects with thin, spiderlike legs skimming over the surface of quiet or gently flowing waters (Figure 68). That insects can swim on the surface of the water is understandable, but how they can run over the surface without getting wet or sinking appears to be rather a mystery.

To explain this strange phenomenon, thoroughly dry a steel needle, then hold it parallel to the surface of some water in a glass tumbler and gently lower it onto the surface so that it floats. By looking carefully you can see how the surface film bends beneath the

We Solve a Mystery

Figure 68
WATER STRIDER

weight of the needle but does not break. Just
how strong the surface film is can be shown
by the following experiment: bend the point
end of a pin to make a hook or use a piece of
fine wire. Sharpen the point of the hook until it is very sharp. Now place your eye on
the level with the surface of the water in the
glass tumbler, place the hook under the surface of the water and gently raise the point
to the surface. If you are careful the point
will not penetrate the surface film but will
lift it slightly upward.

Water striders are able to remain on the
surface for the same reason. Because of their
lightness and of the hairiness of their legs
they exert only a slight pressure on the surface film, only enough to dimple it but not
break it. As we watch them skim over the
surface of a quiet pond or gently flowing

84

brook, drifting with the current, jerking themselves upstream, often jumping and landing again, we can see the dimples they make in the water. These dimples make shadows on the bottom of the pond or brook which draw our attention to the insects as much as the insects themselves.

Water striders often gather in schools in a quiet, sheltered nook or inlet, but scurry for shelter when alarmed. They soon congregate again when all is quiet. In skating on the surface of the water they use the last two pairs of legs, that is, pushing with the middle pair and steering with the last. They use the first pair to capture other insects, dead or living, such as back swimmers, emerging midges that come up from the water below them, and leafhoppers that fall on the water from overhanging shrubs and other plants lining the banks. If you can secure one of these insects, which is not easily done, and examine it carefully with a hand lens, you will observe that the body is covered with soft, velvetlike hairs. These hairs envelop a silvery film of air, enabling the insect to submerge occasionally and to remain for a time beneath the surface.

Water striders pass the winter beneath protecting mudbanks and are often clustered in tangled growths of Chara (Figure 69) and

Figure 69
CHARA

85

Elodea (Figure 23). On warm days they sometimes come out for exercise, so you can collect them throughout the year if you are interested in keeping a few in an aquarium for observation. A light-colored enamel pan with three or four inches of water will do. Although the young and many adults lack wings, the adults of some species have wings and can fly from one pond or stream to another. In order to prevent them from escaping it is best to cover the aquarium or pan with a screen. Sometimes the striders attempt to climb up the sides and in doing so get their feet and bodies wet. As a result they are too heavy to remain on the surface and sink and drown. Therefore it is advisable to provide them with a wooden "shore" nearly flush with the water level or rising gradually out of the water. For this same reason do not use a pail or jar of water in which to carry the striders home; instead use a box containing some damp moss. Feed the striders small insects such as flies, leafhoppers, and the like. They will also take tiny pieces of raw meat.

When collecting striders you may observe scarlet patches on their bodies. These patches are young water mites, which live a parasitic existence on the striders and other water insects until full grown.

DURING the months of May and June swarms of delicate insects may be seen flying about the banks and shores of ponds and streams. They often appear beneath street lights and, if we do not live too far from a pond or stream, about porch lights and window screens. They are beautiful, fragile insects, soft gray and brown or pale and translucent, with large front wings, small hind ones, and with two or three tail filaments. The mouthparts are shrunken, if not actually vestigial, that is, developed or functional at one time but now only rudimentary, and their legs are slender and weak and of little use in walking.

Known as mayflies, these insects live as adults only a few hours or at most a day or two. A few species, however, live several weeks. As adults they live only for the purpose of mating. Once mating has taken place and the females have deposited their eggs in the water they die. Sometimes ponds and streams are strewn with their bodies, which become food for eager fishes.

Although adult mayflies live only a short time, the young live for several years. Called naiads, they occur in many shapes and sizes and have different habits. Some swim about in the water, others run actively over the bottom, still others merely creep. Some sprawl in the mud, others burrow in it. Some

We Get to Know the Mayflies

are found in ponds, others in quiet pools, still others in flowing rivulets or tumbling waterfalls. Whatever their form, habits, and habitats, they all have seven pairs of gills on the abdomen, two or three long, slender tail filaments, and a single claw on each foot. The single claw distinguishes them from stonefly naiads, with which they are sometimes confused. The latter have two claws on each foot and nearly all their gills are on the thorax. Nearly all mayfly naiads are vegetarian, feeding principally on diatoms and desmids, which coat the rocks of a stream bottom and other objects with a golden-green color. They also eat the soft tissues of larger plants. When full grown they shed their skins and emerge from the water as winged adults.

Mayfly naiads, especially those of quiet waters, thrive in an aquarium if well supplied with algae and water plants. They may be collected with a dip net and at any time of the year, even during the winter, although they are not quite as active then as in the summer.

Some species are more common and abundant than others, especially at certain times of the year. During March and April look for Blasturus in spring pools, where hundreds of individuals may be seen swimming about in the water. Chestnut brown with double, leaflike gills, they are nearly full grown and if collected and placed in an aquarium will live for two or three weeks, then shed their skins and emerge and fly to a windowpane. Here they will rest until they have cast their skins for the last time. Mayflies, unlike other insects, molt after they have obtained functional wings.

In ponds and pools where vegetation is plentiful you can find the dainty pale green, brown-dappled Callibaetis (Figure 70). If you can capture naiads with black wing pads they will probably emerge within a few hours after being placed in an aquarium.

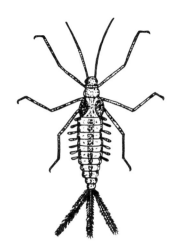

Figure 70
CALLIBAETIS

Naiads of Hexagenia burrow in the muddy shallows of lakes and rivers; sometimes in the banks of upland bog streams. Ungainly creatures when out of their natural habitat, they may be recognized by their bladelike feet, which are admirably adapted for scraping out the mud or sand, and a pair of enormous mandibular tusks projecting forward from beneath the head (Figure 71). Sloping banks are frequently mined by them and in the openings of the burrows their tails may often be seen. Pull out one of the naiads, place it on the mud, and it will burrow in again with a speed that will surprise you.

Figure 71
HEAD OF HEXAGENIA

Similar in appearance but smaller, Ephemera is also a burrower. It frequents smaller

89

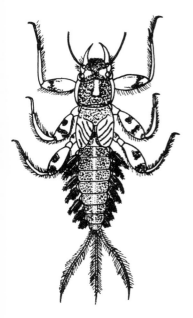

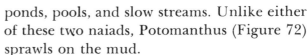

Figure 72
POTOMANTHUS

ponds, pools, and slow streams. Unlike either of these two naiads, Potomanthus (Figure 72) sprawls on the mud.

A different kind of habitat, running water, is preferred by Heptagenia (Figure 73). How well insects may be adapted to a specific habitat is illustrated by Epeorus (Figure 74). The naiads have flattened bodies, knife-blade legs, and grappling claws. All these features are adjustments for living in rapid currents, swift eddies, and waterfalls. Beautiful and delicate insects, they are susceptible to changes in temperature and can survive only a short time in still water.

Perhaps one of the most interesting mayfly naiads is Chirotenetes. A rich chocolate brown with a light median stripe over the head and thorax, it lives in the tumbling

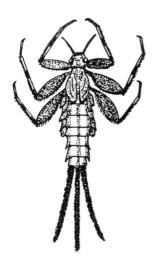

Figure 73
HEPTAGENIA

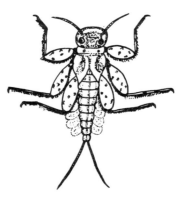

Figure 74
EPEORUS

waters of stony creeks, where it leaps and dashes with considerable agility. Surprisingly, though, it spends most of its time merely sitting on its hind and middle legs, its head up and forefeet held forward. As the current flows by, fringes of long hairs spread out and function as a basket to capture whatever food the current carries. Chirotenetes feeds on a mixed diet of algae and midge larvae, a rare habit among mayflies.

ON A DAY in early March, when the ice of ponds and woodland pools has begun to break up, go to the nearest pond, stand quietly with attentive ears, and you may hear a thin, sweet "pe-ep, pe-ep, pe-ep, pe-ep." It sounds very much like a bird's call note and it seems to come from among the moss and dead leaves at the water's edge. After the four calls, listen, and after a period of silence the calls are repeated. Try to trace the source of the call. You probably won't have much success, for the spring peeper is an elusive little creature and while the air is still chilly remains well hidden. Even though you poke about along the water's edge or examine carefully every stick and bit of grass, he remains a mysterious piping voice.

We Hear Some
Unusual Voices

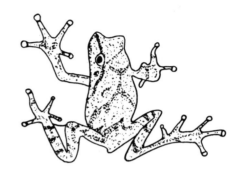

Figure 75
SPRING PEEPER

Return later in the month on a day when the sun shines brightly, the air is balmy, and the golden tassels of the pussy willow sway with every passing breeze. Your solitary peeper has now been joined by others, and their voices are all around you. Again poke about among the moss and leaves, but you still will not find a single peeper.

It is the middle of April. Again return to the pond. This time you will be more successful, and when you arrive at the water's edge you will likely see a little brown body swim vigorously through the water (Figure 75) and climb upon a floating twig. He probably will not remain there very long, but will plunge into the water and swim to the protecting

Figure 76
SPRING PEEPER WITH VOCAL
SAC DISTENDED

cover of floating leaves. He begins singing at
once, and you can see his swollen throat
gleaming like a great white bubble (Figure
76). Another peeper may join him and a
third and a fourth and still others, until
many have joined the chorus. Make a noise
ever so slight. At once there is complete silence. Later in the day, when the sun begins
to sink in the western sky, they sing in ear-
nest, and through the night their high-
pitched chorus can be heard for half a mile
or so.

The singing of frogs and toads in ponds
and marshes is as much a part of our spring
as the return of migratory birds, the appearance of the first wildflowers, and the budding
of trees. The spring peeper, with his shrill,
clear call, is as much a harbinger of spring

93

Figure 77
WOOD FROG

as the bluebird, skunk cabbage, and red maple. To the uninitiated the singing of one species of frog might sound much like that of another, but actually each species has its own distinctive breeding call as well as several other calls.

Consider, for instance, the call of the wood frog (Figure 77). This frog comes out of hibernation shortly after the spring peeper. Sprawling in the shallow water of woodland pools, his head above the surface, he gives voice to a short, sharp, snappy clack. At times two, four, or six notes are given in rapid succession, and when heard close by they sound high, grating, and quite unmusical. Numbers may be found in woodland pools during March and April, and the clacking of the frogs in chorus sounds like the quacking of ducks. Wood frogs are normally shy even during the breeding season, and their clacking ceases immediately when disturbed or alarmed.

In contrast to the shrill note of the peeper is the low, guttural note of the leopard frog, the familiar frog of the marshes, ponds, and cattail swamps. The male frogs, lying in the water half submerged, take a long breath, then suddenly inflate large vocal sacs that gradually distend as the croak resounds. Each croak is a long guttural note, three or more seconds long, followed by from three to six short notes, each a second or less in duration, or the short notes may precede or be interspersed. When singing in chorus the leopard frog repeats the croak four or five times. The sacs remain distended, then suddenly collapse as fresh air is drawn into the lungs. In common with other frogs leopard frogs can croak as well above the surface as below.

The call of the pickerel frog is similar to that of the leopard frog but shorter, somewhat higher-pitched, with a distinct snoring quality. It resembles the sound produced by the tearing of a piece of resistent cloth. About the last of April or around the first of May the isolated calls of the common tree frog (Figure 78) may be heard, and by the middle of May

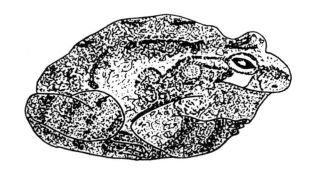

Figure 78
COMMON TREE FROG

they are in full chorus. The call of the tree frog is a loud, resonant trill, ending abruptly, ten or eleven calls in half a minute. The frogs begin calling in the early afternoon, especially on warm, moist days, and continue into the night. With a flashlight and a little patience you can spot any number of the gnomelike males. They do not seem to mind the glare of the flashlight and will continue singing, their pearly, translucent vocal sacs distended into small balloons. If you have never visited a pond at night and watched these little frogs, do so by all means. It is an experience you will remember as long as you live.

Although green frogs (Figure 79) appear in ponds fairly early, they do not begin their croaking until May. The call is an explosive sound and, once heard, is not quickly forgotten. Low-pitched and prolonged, it is likely to be repeated five or six times in succession. Twang a rubber band stretched slightly over an open box and you will have an idea of what it is like. Sometimes when given with less than its usual force it is like the drumming of a woodpecker. The male, when calling, usually sits on a tangled mass of vegetation among grass or water plants or lies sprawled out on the water.

The most distinctive call, one heard in the evenings of early summer, is the sonorous

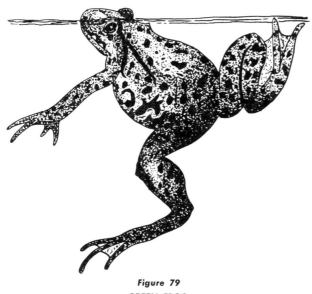

Figure 79
GREEN FROG

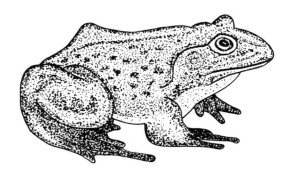

Figure 80
BULLFROG

bass notes of the bullfrog (Figure 80) which
have been translated into "jug-o'-rum, more
rum" or "be drowned, better go round," and
a number of other characterizations. The
bullfrog is the last to come out of hibernation, and it does not begin croaking in the
ponds until nearly June. From that time on,
during the breeding season, a dozen or so
mating pairs can be seen at night in almost
any pond. They may be located with a flashlight, floating outstretched at the surface.

One of the most musical sounds in nature
is the call of the toad. Toads begin to emerge
from their winter burrows in early April. Although an occasional sweet, tremulous call
may be heard issuing from the ponds by the
middle of the month, it is not until the last

98

week of the month that the toad chorus is in full swing. The male does all the vocalizing, giving voice to a long, sustained, high-pitched trill. Hearing it for the first time, you would not suspect that the singer is a toad.

ADVENTURE 20

We Do Some Grafting

CERTAIN FLATWORMS, known as planarians (Figure 81), live in shallow pools, streams, swampy places, ponds, and lakes, in fact in almost any aquatic situation except stagnant water, and preferably in cool, even very cold waters, for temperature is an important environmental factor. Hence, they may be found throughout the year, even in midwinter if the surface of the water is not covered with ice.

Planarians are not called flatworms without reason. They are distinctly flattened. Brown, gray, black, brick red, creamy white, or mottled, according to the species, they are all rather uniform in shape, though some of them have earlike flaps called auricles (Figure 82). The mouth is located near the middle of the ventral surface and opens into a cavity (pharynx sheath) that contains a muscular tube called the pharynx. When feeding planarians extend the pharynx some distance out of the mouth, use it to explore the im-

Figure 81
PLANARIAN

99

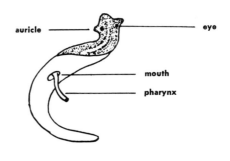

auricle ——————— eye

mouth

pharynx

Figure 82
FLATWORM

mediate surroundings, and then suck food
through it. Normally the pharynx is with-
drawn into the pharynx sheath. The food
taken in through the pharynx passes into a
large, branched intestine sometimes visible
as a vinelike tracery on the back. Undigested
materials are ejected through the mouth as
in the hydra, but the waste products of metabolism are removed by a complex network
of small tubes.

Planarians move in a characteristically slow
gliding fashion over submerged stems, leaves,
and algae-covered stones, the head, which is
always directed forward, bending from side
to side as if "testing" the environment. Touch
or prod a planarian, however, and it moves
quietly away from the region of stimulus by
marked muscular waves. This behavior leads
us to suspect that locomotion is effected by

several methods. The gliding motion is accomplished by numerous cilia located principally on the ventral surface. Besides the cilia the worms have numerous gland cells that open on the surface and secrete a mucous material. This mucous material, a kind of slime, serves as a sidewalk on which they move. The cilia obtain traction on the bed of slime and by their backward action move the animal forward. Planarians are unable to swim and can move only in contact with a solid object or with the underside of the surface film. Planarians have three sets of muscles: longitudinal muscles, which run lengthwise and serve to shorten the animals; circular muscles, which run around the body and constrict them when they contract; and dorsoventral muscles, which flatten them when they contract. These muscles make possible all sorts of agile bending and twisting movements that enable the animal to escape from an unfavorable environmental condition.

Let us collect a few planarians and study their behavior under various conditions. Collecting them is relatively easy, as they cling to sticks, stones, and leaves when these objects are lifted from the water. Examine such objects and if you find any worms attached remove them with the point of a knife. You can also take a mass of vegetation from the water and place it in a pan containing a small amount of water. After a while they will appear on the surface or on the sides of the pan.

Planarians can be kept for short periods in almost any kind of container, a wooden tub, glass bowl, or an enameled pan, but if you want to keep them more or less indefinitely they should be placed in a fish tank containing a shallow bed of clean sand, a few pebbles, and a few water plants. Always use clean water, either from a pond or stream, spring or well. The aquarium or container should be put in a cool place, and, as the animals shun bright light, it should also be darkened with a suitable cover. Planarians can stand neither heat nor lack of oxygen. If they crawl up and form a line along the water's edge their oxygen supply is dangerously low. More plants must then be added or the old water must be replaced with fresh.

Planarians can live for as long as three months or more without food. Under such conditions they live on their own bodies, which gradually decrease in size. They should be fed once or twice a week on beef liver (no other kind), pieces of earthworm, clam, etc., preferably at night, when they are the most active. After two or three hours all uneaten food should be removed, and it is advisable to change the water the day after feeding.

Success in having planarians is a matter of keeping the water clean more than anything else, as they are very susceptible to pollution.

To observe how a planarian feeds, place one upside down in a drop of water and hold a piece of liver within reach. The animal will extend its pharynx through the mouth and suck up the juice until it is ready to burst. Drop a piece of liver into a dish containing several worms and they will quickly congregate on the meat. Planarians have a sense of taste, or, rather, they are sensitive to chemical stimuli and show either a positive or negative response. Put a drop of ammonia or acetic acid in a dish containing several planarians and observe their negative reactions.

Planarians, as a matter of fact, are very sensitive to conditions around them. They dislike bright light, always seeking shadows and dark places, and appear to be able to distinguish between small differences of light. Examine a planarian and you will note a pair of eyes on the dorsal surface near the anterior. These two eyes are sense organs specialized for light reception. Each one consists of black pigment supplied with light-sensitive nerve cells that run to the brain. The pigment shades the nerve cells from light in all directions, but the one from which the light comes. Hence the animal can respond to the source

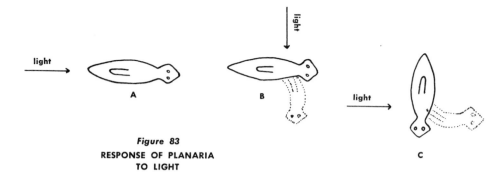

Figure 83
RESPONSE OF PLANARIA
TO LIGHT

of light. You can observe this behavior by a simple experiment. Shine a flashlight on a planarian and it will move away from it, as shown in Figure 83A. Next shine the light at a right angle to the animal (Figure 83B) and it will again move away from it. Shine the light a third time at a right angle and the animal will turn away from it again (Figure 83C).

Planarians are very sensitive to temperature, to touch, and to water currents. Tap the aquarium or container ever so lightly and they will react to the vibration set up by your tapping. That they are sensitive to water currents can be demonstrated by the following experiment. Take a pipette or a piece of glass tubing drawn out to a small nozzle and blow a current of water upon the rear of the worm (Figure 84A). There is no response. Next direct a current of water at the middle of the animal (Figure 84B). Again there is no response. But now direct the current of water

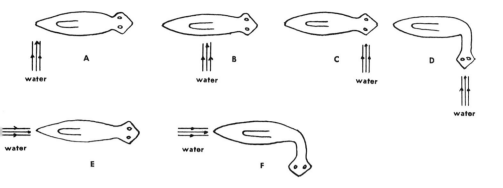

Figure 84
RESPONSES OF PLANARIA
TO WATER CURRENTS

at the head of the animal (Figure 84C). It immediately shows a positive reaction (Figure 84D). The reason for such behavior is that the sensory lobes or auricles, the pointed projections on each side of the head, contain sensory cells sensitive to touch and water currents and presumably to food and chemicals as well. Finally direct a current of water on the animal as shown in Figure 84E. The animal responds as in Figure 84F. The explanation is that the currents from the rear pass along the sides of the body to the sensory lobes and the animal responds by turning its head in the direction of the current. In their natural habitat of streams planarians orient themselves toward the source of the water currents, that is, upstream.

105

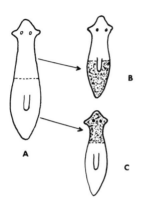

Figure 85
REGENERATION IN PLANARIA.
WORM CUT CROSSWISE.
DOTTED AREAS SHOW
REGENERATED PARTS.

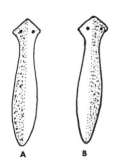

Figure 86
REGENERATION IN PLANARIA.
WORM CUT LENGTHWISE.
DOTTED AREAS SHOW
REGENERATED PARTS.

Some animals have the unique ability to regrow a part of the body that has been lost through injury or accident. Planarians can do this remarkably well. You can observe this power, called regeneration, very easily. You need only a few healthy planarians, a few small, clean dishes, and a knife or razor blade. Place a worm on a glass slide in a shallow dish of water and when it is well extended cut it across the middle (Figure 85A). As planarians lack blood or blood vessels, they cannot be injured by cutting, and as branches of the digestive system ramify in all directions every region can digest food and grow. Place each half of the cut worm in a separate dish; each will regenerate a complete worm, the head a body and the body a head (Figure 85 B, C). Next cut a planarian lengthwise and place each half in a separate dish; again each half will regenerate a complete worm, the right side a left side and the left side a right side (Figure 86A, B). Bear in mind that you have to care for these severed parts as you would for normal planarians, that is, you will have to feed them, keep them dark, and be sure they always have fresh water. Success with your experiment will be determined by conditions; optimum conditions, optimum success, and conversely, if you treat them indifferently, your results will be indifferent.

106

For your next experiment cut a planarian transversely into three, four, or even five pieces and observe what happens. Each section will regenerate a new and complete worm, but you will find that the capacity for regeneration is greatest near the anterior end and decreases toward the posterior end, that is, pieces from the anterior region will regenerate faster and form larger and more normal heads than pieces from the posterior regions. In some species only the pieces from the anterior regions will regenerate a head while pieces from the posterior region will not do so, although they will effect repair. Any piece of the animal usually retains the same polarity it had in the animal. In other words, the head grows out of the cut end of the piece that faced the anterior end in the animal, and the tail grows out of the cut end that faced the posterior end. Some further interesting experiments can be performed by grafting a small piece from one planarian onto another. Cut out a small piece from the head of one as shown in Figure 87A. Make a small wound in the tail of another (Figure 87B) and insert the cut-out piece (graft) in the wound. The grafted piece will grow out into a head (Figure 87C). If the head of one planarian is grafted into another, and then the second one's head is cut off, the grafted head may influence the anterior cut

107

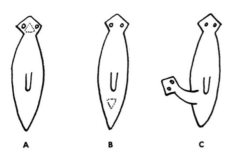

A   B   C

Figure 87

A SMALL PIECE, INDICATED BY
DOTTED LINE, IS CUT FROM
HEAD OF A. THE GRAFT IS
PLACED IN WOUND OF B.
A NEW HEAD DEVELOPS IN C.

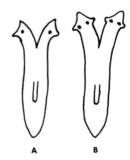

A   B

Figure 88
TWO-HEADED PLANARIA

Figure 89
FIVE-HEADED PLANARIA

surface (which ordinarily would regenerate into a head) to form a tail.

Another experiment to perform is to cut the head of a planarian down the middle into two halves (Figure 88A). A two-headed planarian will result (Figure 88B). If three, four, or five cuts are made, a three-, four-, or five-headed planarian will develop (Figure 89). Repeated cuts may have to be made until complete heads have regenerated, otherwise the cut sections will grow together before new heads have had time to develop. If the cuts are made far enough back each head will form its own pharynx. Depending upon conditions and the nature of the experiment the time needed to conduct these experiments is from several days to several weeks.

108

We Make a Surprising Discovery

PROBABLY no group of animals provides us with so many surprises as the insects. There always seems to be something new to learn from them.

We usually associate insects with the warmer months of the year, spring, summer, and early fall. During the winter they are generally absent except on a warm sunny day when a mourning cloak butterfly flies lazily about in a sunny glade or some flies are warmed into temporary activity but quickly return to their winter quarters when the sun goes down and the air becomes cold again. Certainly we would hardly expect young insects to mature and transform into adults at this time of the year. Surprisingly, certain stone-flies do.

Visit any rapidly flowing stream during any part of the winter and you may find newly emerged adults crawling about on streamside trees and on railings and walls of bridges. Adult stone-flies are flattened, long-bodied, and dull-colored insects, black, brown, or gray, with biting mouthparts and with their wings held flat down their backs, the wide hind ones plaited and hidden beneath the front ones. They are rather inconspicuous, have secretive habits, take to wing awkwardly, and fly slowly. Their flight is so limited they may often be caught by hand. While at rest they may readily be picked up, although when

109

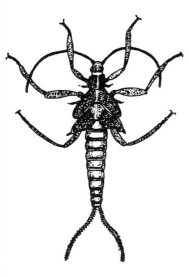

Figure 90
NAIAD OF WINTER STONE-FLY

disturbed they are able to make good their escape by a sort of running gait.

The naiads, with which we are primarily interested, can be found throughout the year in swift water, swirling brooks and waterfalls, never in stagnant water or polluted streams. They are elongate and flattened, in the form of the body resembling the adults, with a pair of tails (cerci) at the end of the body (Figure 90). Most of them have filamentous gills that are always on the lower parts of the body, never on the back or sides, as in mayflies. Stone-fly naiads have two claws on each foot; mayfly naiads have but one. The naiads are often more brightly colored than the adults, with bright greens and yellows in ornate patterns.

Although stone-fly naiads are mainly carnivorous, feeding on mayfly naiads and midge larvae, the winter species are generally herbivorous. You can find the naiads by lifting stones from the water and inverting them. However, since the naiads always seek the dark side of objects the moment the stones are overturned and exposed to light they scatter and drop off the edges into the water. How do they manage to clamber among the rocks and not be swept away by the swift currents? Look at the claws. They are shaped like grappling hooks and can take a firm hold on rocks or other objects. They cling closely to the rocks and lie flat with their legs outspread in a way to present the smallest surface area and the least resistance to the passing current.

Since stone-fly naiads live in well-aerated water, they cannot survive more than a few hours in an aquarium unless they are provided with running water. However, full-grown winter naiads, that is, the naiads about ready to transform, may be collected and kept alive in small vessels containing moist leaves until they emerge as adults. If you want to observe the feeding, mating, and egg-laying habits, transfer the newly emerged adults to an aquarium or wire cage containing a layer of moist sand, a supply of bark bearing a good growth of green algae on which the adults feed, and some old leaves and stems on which they can run around or in which they can hide and rest.

ADVENTURE 22

We Gather a Few Snails

SNAILS are conspicuous and familiar inhabitants of lakes, ponds, and streams, where they occur generally in the shallower parts, since here algae and other water plants that form their main food supply are most abundant. They are mollusks, that is, animals with a soft body and a shell, and unlike the mussels

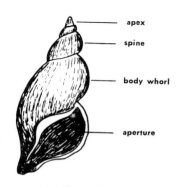

Figure 91
POND SNAIL,
LYMNAEA PALUSTRIS

apex

spine

body whorl

aperture

Figure 92
TADPOLE SNAIL,
PHYSA GYRINA

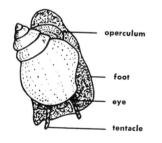

operculum

foot

eye

tentacle

Figure 93
SNAIL SHOWING OPERCULUM

they are great travelers. They move slowly, since they have to carry a heavy load about with them, and there is hardly any level of the shore waters not visited by them. They glide over plants and the surface of any solid object, even the underside of the surface film, from which they often hang suspended. They move through the water on strings of mucus or creep through the mud and bottom ooze. Overturn a floating board or examine a filmy green mass of floating algae and you will probably find dozens of them.

The most conspicuous feature of a snail is its shell, formed by a substance secreted by cells that hardens into a spiral cone. Examine a shell and you will find that it is twisted on an axis called the columella, also that there are lines of growth to show successive additions of new shell. There are right-handed shells and left-handed shells. Hold a shell with its opening, or aperture, toward you and its apex up; if the aperture is at your right the shell is a right-handed one (Figure 91); if at your left it is a left-handed one (Figure 92). Most snail shells are right-handed.

The snail's soft body is twisted and coiled like the shell and extends into the apex. Look at a freshwater snail and you will find it has a distinct head with two tentacles and a small black eye at the base of each (Figure 93).

112

Land snails have four tentacles. Occasionally they wander down to the water's edge and may be picked up for an aquatic one. Snails feed mainly on the soft tissues of plants and the algae occurring on stones which they scrape off with a ribbonlike rasp, or radula (Figure 94). The radula is essentially a flexible file covered with rows of horny teeth and hooks. There is considerable diversity in the shape and arrangement of the teeth and hooks in various species, providing us with the means of classifying them.

Snails move by gliding on a large muscular foot. When in motion wavelike contractions of muscles pass constantly over the bottom of the foot from front to rear. These contractions can be clearly seen as a snail moves over the glass side of an aquarium or beneath the surface film of the water (Figure 95). Some of our freshwater snails breathe by means of gills; others have a lung sac for the purpose. In the gill-bearing snails the blood is supplied with oxygen taken from the water as it passes over the gills. These snails also have a horny plate, the operculum (Figure 93), on the upper surface of the foot, with which they can close the aperture. When a snail completely withdraws within its shell (Figure 96), the operculum entirely fills the aperture and thus gives maximum protection to the animal.

113

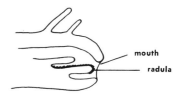

Figure 94
RADULA OF A SNAIL

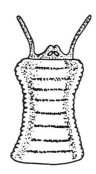

Figure 95
**LOWER SURFACES OF FOOT
AND CONTRACTIONS
OF MUSCLES**

Figure 96
**SNAIL IN PROCESS OF
WITHDRAWING INTO SHELL**

Unlike the gill-bearing snails the air-breathing snails take air into an air chamber or lung sac. These snails are able to take in enough air to last them for a long time underwater. Watch one of these pulmonate snails, as they are called, and you may see an occasional bubble escape from the air chamber when the snail is submerged.

The snails we see oftenest in our ponds and streams are the pond snails, Lymnaea; the pouch or tadpole snails, Physa; and the wheel snails, Planorbis. The pond snails are air-breathing with thin shells, a right-handed whorl, an acute spire, and a large opening, or aperture. They also have a short, rounded foot and flattened, triangular tentacles. A common species, *Lymnaea palustris*, is shown in Figure 91. The shell is elongate conical with an acute apex and six or more whorls. It varies from pale brown to black, with a white thickening on the edge of the opening next to the axis. A related species, *Lymnaea columella* (Figure 97), lives in quiet waters on lily pads and among cattails. It is greenish or yellowish, with four whorls, the last of which forms nearly the entire shell.

Unlike the pond snails, the pouch or tadpole snails are left-handed. The shells are thin, with sharp-pointed spires and with a very large lower whorl. They are very active

Figure 97
LYMNAEA COLUMELLA

114

Figure 98
PLANORBIS TRIVOLVIS

and extremely variable in color. A common species, *Physa gyrina* (Figure 86), has a heavy-looking, thickened, elongate shell with five or six whorls and a loop-shaped opening.

The wheel snails are air-breathing snails with shells that have a flattened spire. The shells may be twisted right or left. An operculum is lacking. A familiar species, living in pools, marshes, and swamps where the water is shallow, is *Planorbis* (Helisoma) *trivolvis* (Figure 98). Popularly called the three-coiled snail, it is one of the larger wheel snails. The shell is yellowish or brown with four whorls, the body whorl elevated above the spire. Common in mats of filamentous algae, on pondweeds, and on thick submerged vegetation, the small *Trivolvis* (Graulus) *parvus* (Figure 99) measures only one-fifth of an inch wide. The shell is yellowish to blackish with four whorls.

Snails with shells shaped like a low cone are called limpets. They are small, about one-

Figure 99
TRIVOLVIS PARVUS

Figure 100
FRESHWATER LIMPET,
ANCYLUS PARELLUS

fifth of an inch long, and live in streams and quiet pools, where they are abundant on vegetation. They are of interest because they have a cone-shaped gill, or pseudobranch, that extends out beyond the shell on the left side in addition to the lung sac. A familiar species occurring on stones and leaves in brooks and ponds is *Ancylus* (Ferrissia) *parellelus* (Figure 100).

Snails live in almost any kind of glass container, even a glass tumbler, but if they are to be kept over a long period of time more permanent quarters, such as an aquarium, should be provided. Species that live in marshes and swamps should have only about two or three inches of water, those that inhabit ponds and streams ten to twelve inches. Water from the snail's own habitat is preferable, but if this is not convenient, water from a pond or stream. Tap water should never be used.

The aquarium, which should be placed in a subdued light and covered with a piece of glass to exclude dust and gases, should contain a layer of sand and pebbles and be planted with various kinds of water plants such as Elodea, Nitella (Figure 22), and Myriophyllum. Some filamentous algae might also be added, as this is a source of both oxygen and food. Dead leaves and small sticks covered

116

with microscopic plants can be introduced from time to time, the sticks being so arranged to serve as highways for use in reaching the surface for air. Snails seem to be fond of lettuce leaves, and small sections can be given occasionally. Since calcium carbonate is essential to maintain the acidity of the water as well as to provide lime for the shells, a pinch or two of cuttlefish bone should be dropped into the water at intervals.

Given the proper conditions, snails will thrive and live in an aquarium the year round. They will also mate and lay their eggs. Many snails deposit their eggs in masses of an amber-colored protective jelly that may be attached to the plants or the glass sides. The developing embryos can be seen clearly through the jellylike mass. They turn over and over within their capsules, and their black eyes and characteristic snail humps may easily be discerned with a hand lens. In order to rear the young snails they should, upon hatching, be transferred to a separate jar of water of the same temperature containing some algae for oxygen supply; otherwise they are apt to be eaten by the adult snails. They can be fed dried, powdered lettuce leaves or finely powdered tropical-fish food sprinkled on top of the water. Once the snails have passed the early stages of development, they

117

can be given the same fare as the adults.

What determines whether a snail is to be right-handed (dextral) or left-handed (sinistral)? By breeding experiments it has been shown that the direction of coiling is an inherited trait; in other words, in a species where dextrality is normal it is inherited as a simple Mendelian dominant to sinistrality, and conversely, in a species where sinistrality is normal it is also inherited as a simple Mendelian dominant. The question now arises, are there deviations from the normal in any given species? The answer is in the affirmative. For some reason there appears to be a higher percentage of deviation among terrestrial snails than among marine species.

An interesting project can be developed to determine the degree of abnormality in our freshwater snails. Species of Lymnaea that are normally dextral and species of Physa that are normally sinistral provide excellent material for such an undertaking. Empty shells can be gathered and taken home for study, or the living snails can be examined in the field and returned to the water. There is no need to kill them to determine the direction of twisting. If any abnormal snails are found, they may be taken home to serve as the beginning of some interesting breeding experiments.

SOMETIME during the summer peek into a roadside puddle or a temporary pool and you will probably see the immature stages of the mosquito. We are apt to dismiss the mosquito as a nuisance, which it is, but the insect is of more than passing interest, as it illustrates a successful adaptation to an aquatic habit.

Collect some of the larvae and pupae and place them in a glass of water (Figure 101). The larvae can be recognized by their wriggling motion as they swim through the water. Hence they are popularly known as "wrigglers." Examine one with a hand lens. It has a large head and thorax and a slender, tapering abdomen (Figure 102). Note the tufts of hairs, or setae, on the antennae and on the segments of the abdomen, characters much used in the classification of mosquito larvae. On the next to the last segment there is a long, straight tube, and at the end of the last

We Peek into a Roadside Puddle

Figure 101
TUMBLER OF WATER
CONTAINING LARVAE AND
PUPAE OF MOSQUITO

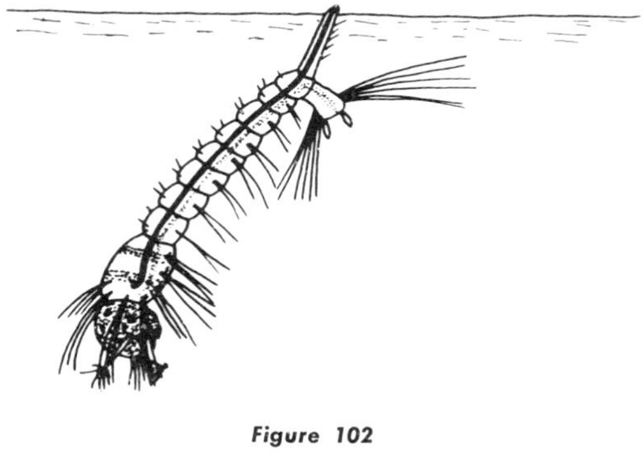

Figure 102
LARVA OF MOSQUITO

abdominal segment one or two pairs of tracheal gills. The tube is a breathing organ and has at the tip a pair of spiracles armed with a rosette of hairs. When at rest at the surface of the water, the breathing tube is extended above the surface and the rosette of hairs is spread out on the surface film, helping to support the larva.

Although the food of mosquito larvae varies with the species, most of them feed on organic matter suspended in the water or floating on the surface. When feeding the larvae use a remarkable set of jaws armed with brushes. By moving the brushes rapidly currents of water are created and bring food to the mouth. The larvae propel themselves through the water by undulatory movements of the abdomen. They also employ the tracheal gills, which consist of four fingerlike processes and tufts of hairs. Watch the larvae carefully as they swim. They swim "tail" first. The gills take hold of the water and pull them backward. The wrigglers do not remain below the surface of the water very long, since it is essential that they take in fresh air often.

The pupae (Figure 103) are unlike the larvae in form. They are humped-up little creatures that remind us of a question mark. The head and thorax are greatly enlarged and are not distinctly separated; the abdomen

120

Figure 103
PUPA OF MOSQUITO

is slender and flexible. During the transition from the larval to the pupal stage a remarkable change takes place in the respiratory system. The single breathing tube of the larva is replaced by two earlike appendages (breathing tubes) situated on the thorax. They look like a pair of horns. When the pupa is at rest, the head remains upright so the breathing tubes can be extended above the surface of the water. At the tip of the abdomen there is a pair of leaflike appendages used in swimming. The pupa, unlike the pupae of most other insects, is active. However, the pupae usually do not move unless disturbed. They do not eat.

The pupal stage is brief, usually not more than two or three days. When transformation is complete, the skin splits down the back and the winged mosquito works its way out carefully and then cautiously balances itself on the cast skin, using it as a raft, until its wings are hardened and it can fly away.

Perhaps you would like to breed the adults and complete the life cycle. Breeding experiments are best carried on in a large container such as a fish aquarium, which should be covered with mosquito netting or some other suitable material so the adult mosquitoes will not fly away. Transfer the pupae to the aquarium and float some small splinters of wood on the surface for the adults to rest on. When the adults have emerged they must be fed until they have mated and the female has deposited her eggs. The males, which can be distinguished from the females by their plumose antennae, do not suck blood, but feed on plant juices. Small pieces of fruit may be placed on the surface for them. It has been found that the best food for the males is cooked raisins. Place a small quantity of raisins—the large varieties are the most satisfactory—in a pan, cover with water, and boil until almost dry. Then replenish the water and continue boiling until the raisins are suspended in their own syrup. They may be kept in a refrigerator and one or two placed on top of the mosquito netting every few days. These raisins, if kept moist, should last for a week or so.

Although the females may be fed on diets other than blood, such as egg yolk and potato, carrot and apple juices, they are more likely to mate and oviposit if they are provided with blood. Small pieces of juicy raw meat can be placed on the wood splinters.

If all goes well the females will lay their eggs on the surface of the water. In our common species the eggs resemble small cartridges and are placed side by side in an upright position so the entire cluster looks like a small raft (Figure 104). When the eggs hatch the young wrigglers may be fed on a variety of substances. One of the best appears to be dry skim milk. It should be added to the water daily from the time of hatching, in very small amounts at first, but the amounts can be increased gradually. The amount to give them can only be learned through experience.

Breeding mosquitoes is relatively easy if attention is paid to their essential requirements. The best temperature for breeding experiments is about 80° F., and the water should not be allowed to get cloudy or turbid. The eggs of some species hatch very soon after

Figure 104
EGGS OF MOSQUITO

they are laid, but in the majority of species the winter is passed in the egg stage. If the eggs laid in your aquarium do not hatch within a few days, you probably do not have the right species. So try again. Given the right species and the right conditions, mosquitoes should complete their life cycle in a short time, say within two weeks.

ADVENTURE 24

We Ask a Question

IF YOU HAVE EVER watched whirligig beetles, you will agree that they have been well named. The whirligigs are the small steel-blue or black beetles that may be seen in brooks and the quiet waters of ponds, swimming about in circles (Figure 105).

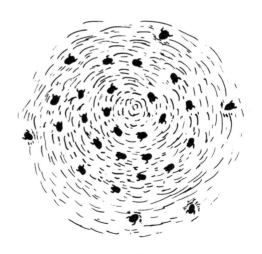

Figure 105
WHIRLIGIGS SWIMMING IN CIRCLES ON POND SURFACE

The next time you see these beetles watch them for a while and notice, as they dart around and around each other, whether they ever bump into one another or any other object. You will find that no matter how fast they swim or how many there are on the pond they never collide. Even if transferred to an aquarium there are still no collisions. How do they manage to avoid each other?

The logical conclusion is that they see each other, but darken a room and illuminate the aquarium with the red light of a dark-room lamp, such as a photographer uses and to which the beetles do not react, and they still will not collide. However, remove all dust from the surface of the water by skimming it several times with the sharp edge of a glass plate, or coat the inside walls of the aquarium with paraffin so that the water meniscus disappears, and they will not only collide with one another but also bump into the glass walls.

The explanation of why they avoid collisions is that the beetles detect vibrations of moving particles on the surface of the water, set into motion by their own movements, and by vibrations reflected from various objects in the water and from the shore. The organ* that appears to be sensitive to these vibrations

* Johnston's organ.

is a complex structure composed mainly of tactile hairs and located in the second segment of the antennae; if this segment is cut from the antennae, collisions occur.

Many interesting moments can be spent watching whirligigs in an aquarium, but you will have to catch them first. They are surprisingly agile and will thwart every attempt to being caught, evading a net with an uncanny ability and even when caught with a net often escaping from it by springing out of it. When handled they emit a milky fluid with a rather peculiar odor that is probably a defensive device, though they do not seem in need of any defensive weapon.

As the whirligig beetles like plenty of room in which to swim, a wide aquarium is preferable to a narrow one. It need not be particularly deep—a shallow one will do. They breathe atmospheric air, and therefore oxygenating plants are not necessary. However, a few should be placed in the aquarium to provide a support for the beetles when they dive. Since they can fly well, if they can climb out of the water, the aquarium should be covered with a screen top, mosquito netting, or similar material.

Examine a beetle carefully (Figure 106) and you will see why it is such a capable swimmer. The body is oval, flattened, and smooth, thus

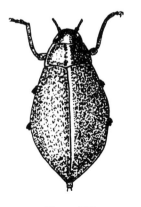

Figure 106
WHIRLIGIG BEETLE

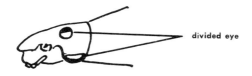

divided eye

Figure 107
HEAD OF WHIRLIGIG,
SHOWING DIVIDED EYE

helping to reduce water resistance. In some species the ventral side is shaped like a canoe, permitting the insect to move through the water with even greater ease. The hind legs are paddle-shaped and fringed with hairs and serve as efficient propelling organs, being used as oars to drive them through the water in a rapid sculling movement. Look closely at their eyes with a hand lens and you will find that they are divided by the sharp margins of the head so they look up from the water with one eye and down into it with another (Figure 107). They frequently dive, and when they do so carry down with them a bubble of air at the tips of and under the wing covers.

The whirligigs in the aquarium will eat mayfly naiads, pieces of earthworms, mealworms, and small pieces of raw meat. Drop a piece of food in the midst of half a dozen or so of these beetles and a merry battle will ensue. They will all crowd around it, each tearing off a mouthful and devouring it with avidity.

Whirligigs will breed in captivity if some

127

Figure 108
CRYSTALWORT, RICCIO

Figure 109
DUCKWEED

Figure 110
LARVA OF WHIRLIGIG BEETLE

floating crystalwort (Figure 108) or duckweed (Figure 109) is provided on which to deposit their eggs. The larvae (Figure 110), which look like small centipedes, thrive on mayfly naiads. When full grown they emerge from the water by climbing up water plants and spin grayish pupal cases that they attach to the plants. The aquarium should contain a layer of sand to serve as anchorage for the plants as well as for a surface on which the larvae can crawl, since in their native habitat they spend much of their time crawling over the bottom trash of ponds and brooks, though they also swim through the water with a sinuous motion of their bodies.

In late may and in June look for a shallow area in a pond or stream and keep it under observation—you may see the sunfish build his nest (Figure 111).

Although fishes are not normally associated with nest building, we have seen that the stickleback builds one that resembles a bird's nest (Adventure 16) and is an elaborate nest for a fish. Other fishes that build them do not go to such lengths. The sunfish, for instance, merely clears a circular space on the bottom

We Spy on the Sunfish

Figure 111
SUNFISH BUILDING NEST

of the pond or stream about a foot or so in diameter and about an inch deep. He removes the gravel with his tail, the larger stones with his mouth. The result is a basinlike clearing. Although it may not seem much of a nest, it serves his purpose.

When the nest is ready for use, the male seeks a mate. Together they swim around in circles over the clearing, their ventral sides close together while the eggs and sperms are discharged into the water. As soon as the eggs are fertilized, they drop to the bottom and become attached to small stones or to the roots of plants uncovered by the male during his excavating activities. The female's sole duty is to lay eggs, and once her role in the reproductive act has been completed she swims away and leaves the male to guard and attend first the eggs and then the developing young. He performs the task faithfully, occasionally fanning the embryos with his tail so they may get enough oxygen. If the temperature of the water is within the range of 60° to 75° F., the eggs hatch in from two to six days.

If you are unable to watch the nest-building and mating activities of the sunfish in its native habitat, you may be able to do so in an aquarium. If you are not acquainted with this familiar fish of our ponds, a few words of description will help you to recognize it. It has a flat body shaped like a seed of a pump-kin and therefore popularly known as the pumpkinseed. The back is an olive green delicately shaded with blue, the sides are spotted with orange, the belly a bright yellow, and the cheeks are orange color striped with many lines of blue. Near the edge of the gill cover is a bright scarlet spot. The male is more handsomely marked than the female and has black ventral fins; those of the female are yellowish. The male's dorsal and caudal fins are also a more brilliant blue.

As adults, sunfish may be fed chopped raw fish, small sections of earthworms, or pieces of freshly ground raw beef. If you are successful breeding your fishes and having eggs hatch, give the young Daphnia (See Adventure 35), hard-boiled egg yolk, finely chopped worms, raw beef juice, and fine tropical-fish food three times a day and vary the foods among those mentioned, with emphasis on the Daphnia and worms. When about five weeks old the young can be given adult fare. As adult sun-fish sometimes show cannibalistic tendencies, it is advisable to remove them from the aquar-ium when the young hatch. The aquarium should contain a layer of sand, have enough oxygenating plants, and be covered with a piece of glass to exclude dust. It should also be fairly large. Be sure to check with your local game laws, as you may need a fishing license to collect native fishes.

ADVENTURE 26

We Learn about Countershading

HAVE YOU EVER noticed how fishes are generally darker on the back and sides and lighter on the lower surface and that many shore birds are similarly colored? Seen from above, the fishes blend with the dark bottom of the pond or stream and the birds with the sand of the beach. Equally when the fishes and birds are viewed from below against the light color of the sky, both are almost invisible. Both fishes and shore birds are darkest above where they receive the most light and lightest below where they receive the most shadow. This type of concealing coloration is known as countershading.

The back swimmer (Figure 112) is a common inhabitant of our ponds and streams. We usually find it resting at the surface, floating head downward, with the tip of its abdomen extended above the surface into the air and its long hind legs outstretched like oars or sweeps ready to propel the insect through the water for food or to safety should danger threaten. The insect is shaped like an overturned boat and has the unique ability of being able to swim on its back. Unlike those

132

of the fishes and birds, the back of the insect is of a pearly color and the lower surface, which is dark, is uppermost and blends with the bottom mud and sand, while the lighter back, when seen from below, blends with the sky. Possibly this coloration helps the insect to capture its food and to escape being a victim itself.

Although the tip of its abdomen is extended above the surface of the water, the insect does not have a breathing tube, as does the water scorpion or the larva and pupa of the mosquito, but takes in air through hair-covered channels and spiracles on the thorax. It is an expert diver and when alarmed descends to the bottom, carrying down with it a silver film of air on the ventral surface of the body. Being

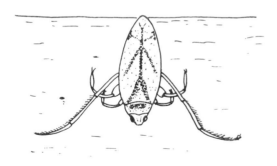

Figure 112
BACK SWIMMER

lighter than water, it must hold onto a plant stem or other object to remain submerged. The strong, grasping front legs are admirably suited as anchors and for grasping prey, from which it sucks the body juices by means of its suctorial beak. This beak can inflict a burning sting, so be careful when you handle the insect, since the effect of the sting may last for some time should you be susceptible to insect poison.

Back swimmers, which can be collected with a net or any kind of scoop, do well in captivity, and several of them may be kept in an aquarium or jar deep enough for them to dive. A few plants should be included to provide them with a means of remaining submerged. Observe how effective their hind legs are as oars and how they capture their prey. They can be fed small water insects such as mosquito larvae, small sections of earthworms, and tiny bits of raw meat. As back swimmers can fly, the aquarium or jar should be covered with mosquito netting or similar material.

ADVENTURE 27

We Study Some Worms

NOT MANY OF US are interested in worms. They seem drab, colorless, uninteresting. However, they play a significant role in the

134

economy of nature, and some are the causative agents of various diseases. We are not concerned in this adventure with the earthworms, of much value to agriculture, or with the parasitic worms that cause disease, but rather with a group of worms called the bristleworms, or oligochaetes, found in ponds and lakes and in the still waters of coves and stagnant, muddy, or marshy pools where there is an abundance of submerged and decaying vegetation.

The bristleworms known as naids (family Naidae) are small, measuring about half an inch in length, with slender, cylindrical bodies divided into segments clearly defined on the outside by constrictions and set off internally by muscular partitions. Tufts of chitinous rods called setae, or bristles, occur on the segments in varying numbers and differ in length and form.

Collecting naids is an easy matter. By simply rinsing freshly gathered algae and water plants in a dish of clean water hundreds of these worms that were hiding among the plants can be uncovered. The worms that live in the bottom mud can be collected by scooping up the mud and screening it through a fine-meshed net or sieve. One of the commoner bristleworms is the graceful, transparent little worm known as Nais (Figure

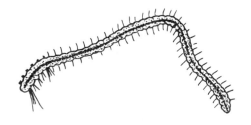

Figure 113
NAIS

113). It lives in the mud or among algae or on the leaflets of various water plants. Whitish or yellowish in color, it is free-swimming, moving about with the aid of its bristles, which are usually longer toward the anterior end. Chaetogaster (Figure 114), another bristleworm, is somewhat larger than most and creeps about on its dense bristle clusters. Then there is the lively little Dero (Figure 115), hardly a quarter of an inch long. It lives in a

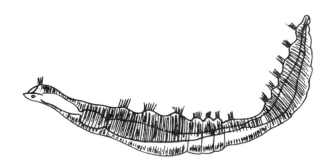

Figure 114
CHAETOGASTER

tube on the surface of lily pads and duckweed and slips in and out of its tube, even changing ends within it, with astonishing speed. All these bristleworms reproduce by budding, that is by automatic division of the body, and frequently chains of incompletely formed worms result.

Another family of worms is the Tubificidae. The worms are slender, from one-half to one and a half inches in length, and are not free-swimming, but live in tubes that they build in the mud. The tubes are in part burrows and in part chimneys that extend above the surface of the surrounding mud. The tails, which extend out of the tubes, are in constant motion and when viewed closely look like waving fringes (Figure 116). When alarmed the worms disappear within their tubes. The bodies of these worms are so transparent that the coloring matter of the blood, erythrocruorin, shows through their skin. Hence they are popularly known as blood-worms. When they are thickly associated, the mud in which they live assumes a reddish color.

Tubifex, the common species, feeds on decaying organic matter that it obtains by digging its head an inch or more down into the mud. All waste matter is ejected from the tail. By overturning the bottom mud of ponds

Figure 115
DERO

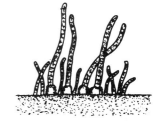

Figure 116
TUBIFEX

Tubifex works much as the earthworm does in tilling the soil of the land.

If you have a microscope or have access to one, you can see the heartbeat of Tubifex. Observe the single pair of aortic arches, or loops, and note the movement of the dorsal blood vessel, which pumps the blood. If the worms move about too much, they may first be anesthetized by placing them in a drop of water to which a drop of very dilute formaldehyde has been added.

ADVENTURE 28

We Capture Some Water Mites

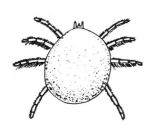

Figure 117
WATER MITE

IN QUIET WATERS of a stream and in permanent still pools small specks of red, orange, green, yellow, brown, or blue may be seen any time of the year swimming swiftly through the water, even beneath the ice in winter. The dictionary defines a mite as anything small, a small object, a particle. What better word fits these animated colored specks? All we need do is add the word water and we have the name of these minute animals (Figure 117).

Water mites are rotund or oval in form and rarely measure more than a quarter of an inch in length. One of the largest is about a third of an inch long, but most of them are barely larger than the head of a pin. The

138

skin is usually soft and easily broken. The upper surface may be entirely smooth, have a few scattered fine bristles, or be densely clothed with short hairs. The eyes, two or four in number, are generally on the upper surface near the front border and are rather small.

Water mites breathe air. On the ventral surface is one or more very small dark spots. They are the external openings of the air tubes, or tracheae, that ramify throughout the body and supply it with oxygen. Although the water mites breathe air, they can submerge and remain beneath the water for long periods.

Water mites are active and either run about on the surface film or submerge and swim through the water. They are propelled by their eight legs, which are fringed with hairs to aid in swimming. The strokes are made in rapid succession and have the effect of moving the animal smoothly forward. Quite often they descend to the bottom, where they creep about on the mud and sand and over submerged plants. They are carnivorous and clutch their prey, from which they suck the body juices. The mouth is a complicated organ with short jointed palpi, or feelers.

The eggs are small brownish jelly masses attached to the stems of water plants or to the lower surfaces of floating leaves. They are also deposited on the gills of mussels, sponges, and the bodies of aquatic insects such as the water striders (See Adventure 17). The larvae live a parasitic existence until full grown, when they become free-living. Newly hatched larvae have only six legs and pass through several molts before they take the form of adults.

Water mites are fairly abundant in early spring but occur in the greatest numbers in late summer and autumn. They can be easily captured with a net or by submerging a bottle and allowing some of the water plants to float into it. Mites hiding among them will be carried along. For some reason they do not do well in captivity and will live only a short time in an aquarium.

One of our common species is Eylais. It has a red oval body, measures about an eighth of an inch in length, and has long legs. Another species, also with an oval body and dark red with dark spots on the back, is Hydrachna. It is one of the largest of the water mites and is usually common in swamps and ponds. The species whose young we find attached to water striders is Limnochares. This mite is also red but has a rectangular body. Look for it on bottoms of ponds, where it may be seen walking over the mud and submerged plants.

WHEN COLLECTING WORMS you may sometimes gather in wormlike animals as those shown in Figure 118, and assume that they are species of worms. To the naked eye they look like worms. But look at them with a hand lens and compare them with the worms and you will observe differences. They have distinct heads, almost hairless bodies, and fleshy prolegs at each end of the body. Prolegs are never found on worms.

The wormlike animals, the larvae of certain insects called midges, are found in the muddy, trashy bottoms of pond shallows and along the weed-grown banks of slow-moving streams. Some of them live in tubes that they make out of bits of sediment, dead leaves, or particles of sand, held together by a cement-like secretion from certain glands. The tubes are attached to the surfaces of dead leaves, stems, sticks, and stones, in fact any solid object (Figure 119). They are generally soft and fragile and are never portable; new ones

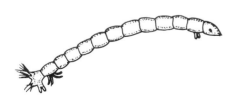

Figure 118
CHIRONOMUS, A MIDGE
LARVA

Figure 119
TUBES OF MIDGE LARVAE

are made whenever the larvae are obliged to leave the old ones. Dead leaves of ponds and pools are frequently covered with a network of these tubes, and if you transfer a handful of the leaves to a collecting dish and let the "catch" stand for a while, you will find the sides of the dish covered with them.

Species of Chironomus (Figure 118) build tubes in the soft mud of pond bottoms. The best known are a brilliant red and are called bloodworms, a name also given to the Tubifex worms. They need not be mistaken for one another, as the midge larvae have a distinct head and prolegs, as mentioned above. Examine a Chironomus larva with a hand lens and you will observe two pairs of long "blood gills" on the eleventh segment. These gills are thin-walled sacs into which the blood from the body flows freely.

As insignificant-appearing as the midge larvae may appear to be, they are of considerable importance in the economy of nature. They live on algae and decayed vegetation and on such a diet they thrive and multiply in great numbers. In turn they are preyed upon extensively by all kinds of aquatic animals: predacious insects, young fishes, and other aquatic carnivores. As a matter of fact, they constitute a staple fish food.

Midge larvae can easily be reared into adult

midges; indeed the entire life cycle can be carried out in an enameled pan within a period of from four to five weeks. Should you wish to do so, fill an enameled pan with pond water to a depth of about an inch or two and cover the bottom with mud taken from the same pond or pool where you collect the larvae. Transfer the larvae to the pan and feed them on a diet of milk. A few trials will tell you just how much to give them. Do not change the water, but add a little each day to replace that which evaporates. Keep the water at a temperature of about 65° F. and do not allow it to become murky and smell.

The pupal stage is usually passed in the same tubes occupied by the larvae. The pupae resemble those of the mosquito. They have a large thorax from which respiratory horns or tufts extend upward like ears and take in air. To prevent the adult midges from escaping, cover the pan with a screening of some sort.

To MOST OF US salamanders are more of a word than actual living animals. The main reason is that they are generally secretive and for the most part remain hidden from view during the daylight hours. One exception, however, is a small salamander known as the

ADVENTURE 30

We Attend a Ritual

Figure 120
COMMON NEWT

spotted newt (Figure 120), which is active
during the day in ponds and streams. It is a
common species throughout the Eastern part
of the country and may be seen from spring
to fall swimming in almost any pond and in
quiet stretches of meandering streams.

Adult newts vary in size in different local-
ities and even in different waters of the same

general locality, but they usually measure three to four inches in length, the male being somewhat larger than the female and with larger hind legs. The color is variable, but on the upper surface it is usually olive green, varying through shades of yellowish brown to dark greenish brown. The lower surface or underparts vary from light to bright yellow. Black spots are scattered irregularly over both surfaces and range from minute points to blotches of considerable size. Along each side of the back is a row of scarlet dots ringed with black. During the breeding and mating season, in March and April, horny black ridges appear on the inner surface of the male's hind legs and horny black excresences on the ends of the toes. The tail of the male also becomes conspicuously broadened and the vent, or cloaca, quite protuberant.

The courtship of the newt is most interesting, and if possible the mating activites of the animal should be observed. The male begins to woo the female by moving stealthily toward her with an air of exaggerated caution. On seeing him approach the female darts away quickly in a state of considerable agitation. The male again approaches the female and again she darts away. Unwearied, the male continues his advances. During all this maneuvering a colorless substance secreted by glands in his cheeks has been expelled into the water. This substance gradually exercises a sort of hypnotic effect on the female, and at last she allows the male to approach, whereupon he becomes greatly excited and performs a series of contortions. Suddenly he vaults onto the back of the female and grasps her tightly around her body with his strong hind legs. He then bends his body in an S-shaped curve and rubs the side of his head against hers, at the same time tapping his tail against her body. In this position a period of quiet follow that may last from thirty minutes to several hours, both animals remaining motionless except for the fanning of the tail.

At last the male passes into a violent stage and begins to drag and shake the female, meanwhile quivering with intense excitement. At this time the cloaca of the male begins to swell and a few whitish papillae begin to project from the sides. Suddenly, after a few rapid bendings of his body from side to side, the male lets go of the female and moves a short distance away. If the female follows him, he deposits a white, vase-shaped spermatophore (Figure 121) containing spermatozoa, whereupon the female crawls over it and takes the mass of sperm cells into her cloaca. Here the eggs are fertilized. The female lays her eggs singly, each in a capsule

Figure 121
SPERMATOPHORE

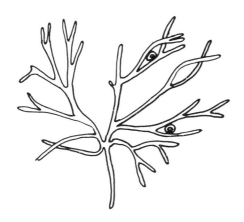

Figure 122
EGGS AMONG LEAVES
OF HORNWORT

of jelly and fastened to the stem or leaf of a
water plant (Figure 122). They are brown at
one end, creamy or light green at the other,
and as many as several hundred may be laid
by one female. As only a few eggs are deposited each day, egg-laying is a drawn-out
process and may cover an extended period.

Since newts thrive in captivity and will
breed in an aquarium, it is not necessary to
visit a pond to watch their courtship. They
are best kept in a semiaquatic terrarium,
which is an aquarium containing several
inches of water and one end of which is built
up with rocks, coarse gravel, and woods loam

147

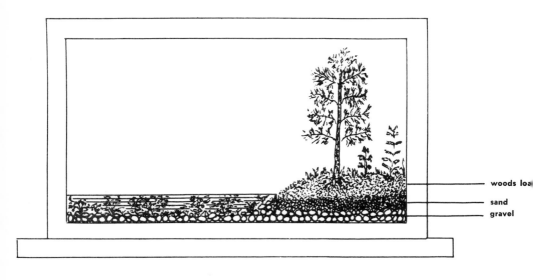

woods loa[m]
sand
gravel

Figure 123
SEMIAQUATIC TERRARIUM

in which various plant forms such as small white pine, cedar, and hemlock seedlings, wintergreen, club mosses, ferns, and mosses are planted (Figure 123). The terrarium should not be exposed to the direct rays of the sun during the middle part of the day; if placed in a window where direct sunlight will strike it, the light can be diffused with a curtain drawn across the window. The temperature should be maintained in the vicinity of 75° F. in the daytime, with a drop during the night to about 60° F. Newts are carnivorous and feed on midges, mosquito larvae, mayfly naiads, small insects such as aphids and tree-

148

hoppers that fall on the surface of the water from trees and shrubs and other plants that grow near the banks of ponds, as well as snails and small crustaceans. In addition to these items they can also be given finely ground pieces of fresh beef, liver, and sections of earthworms.

The eggs of the newts hatch in about a month, depending on the temperature of the water. In their natural habitat the larvae usually emerge in May. They are about five-eighths of an inch long, light yellowish green in color, with a faint gray line on each side of the spine. The newly hatched larvae have branching gills, "balancers," buds of their front legs, which rapidly elongate within a few days, and fishlike tails. Toward fall they gradually lose their gills and acquire lungs and their color changes from green to red. Other changes occur, such as loss of the dorsal keel and tail fins. Following these transformations the young, now known as "efts," leave the ponds and take to land, where they live for several years. Then they return to the water, assume the coloration of the adults, and mate, thus completing their life cycle. The spotted newt has therefore two stages and two color phases in its life history, the olive-green aquatic phase and the red land stage.

If you are successful in getting your newts

to mate, it is advisable to transfer the eggs to a separate terrarium so that when they hatch the larvae will not be eaten by the adults. During the development of the newt embryo and also on hatching you can see the circulation of the blood with a hand lens. When the larvae transform into the efts, they may be fed the same fare as the adults.

ADVENTURE 31

We Catch Some Giants

Sometimes in our choice of adjectives we exaggerate, but no one can dispute the choice of the word "giant" when applied to a certain group of aquatic insects known as the giant water bugs, for in comparison to most other water insects they are truly gigantic, some of them measuring as much as two inches long, while some tropical species attain a length of four inches.

The giant water bugs are wide, flat-bodied, oval, brownish or grayish insects and are very predacious. Their front legs are raptorial and are admirably suited for catching prey; the middle and hind legs, flattened and oarlike, are adapted for swimming; and at the tip of the abdomen is a pair of narrow, straplike respiratory appendages that are retractile.

We do not expect such insects to be capable flyers, but they do take to wing and fly strongly

and for great distances. Some species are attracted to electric lights, where they congregate in considerable numbers. They are called
electric light bugs.

One of our commoner species, Benacus,
is shown in Figure 124. It is a facile master
of the pond and quiet pool and hides beneath
stones or other objects to await the approach
of a minnow, frog, or some other small animal. With astonishing speed it issues forth
from its vantage point, grasps the unsuspect-
ing prey with its strong clasping forelegs, and
plunges its deadly beak deep into the flesh of
the hapless victim, whose blood it sucks. Be
careful when you capture this water bug, because it can inflict a painful wound.

The eggs of Benacus are large, curiously
streaked or striped (Figure 125), and are attached in clusters two or three inches long to
various water plants. The eggs are so large
that the hatching of the young can be clearly
seen with the naked eye. I would suggest that
you look for the egg clusters and transfer the
plant stalks containing them to an aquarium
so that you can watch the entire process.
Observe that each egg has a cap at the free
end which the young water bug loosens when
ready to emerge. The line along which the
cap opens in indicated on the egg shell by a
white crescent-shaped streak.

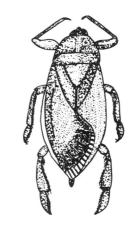

Figure 124
GIANT WATER BUG, BENACUS

Figure 125
EGG OF BENACUS

151

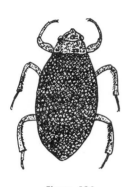

Figure 126
WATER BUG, BELOSTOMA,
CARRYING EGGS

The adult water bugs thrive in an aquarium or even in a dish of water if they are well supplied with food, such as insects and pond snails, but be sure that the aquarium or dish is covered with a piece of screening; otherwise the water bugs are apt to escape.

The females of certain species of the giant water bugs, Belostoma, have a curious habit of placing their eggs on the backs of the males. When the female is ready to deposit her eggs, she mounts on top of the male and attaches her eggs, which may number a hundred or more, to his back with a waterproof glue she secretes for the purpose. The male vigorously protests such behavior, but to no avail. The eggs are carried about by the male for ten days or more or until they hatch (Figure 126). It is an odd sight to see the male transporting his burden of eggs, and it would be well worth keeping an eye out for him.

ADVENTURE 32

We Venture into Animal Husbandry

FOR A LONG TIME sponges were something of an enigma. They were variously believed to be plants, animals, a combination of both, and even a nonliving substance. About a hundred years ago their animal character was definitely established.

To most of us today a sponge is a synthetic,

152

and if we think of natural sponges at all the bath sponge comes to mind. Most natural sponges are generally associated with tropic seas, but they are found in cooler seas of northern latitudes and in our ponds and streams.

If we examine a living freshwater sponge (Figure 127) with a hand lens, we find that it has a rough surface peppered with numerous holes or pores; hence the name of the group Porifera (pore-bearing), to which the sponges belong. The holes are the openings of a network of canals and chambers (Figure 128) through which water flows, the small pores (ostioles) being the external openings of the incurrent canals through which water enters, and the large pores (oscula) being the external openings of the excurrent canals through which water leaves the sponge. The water is made to flow through the canals and chambers

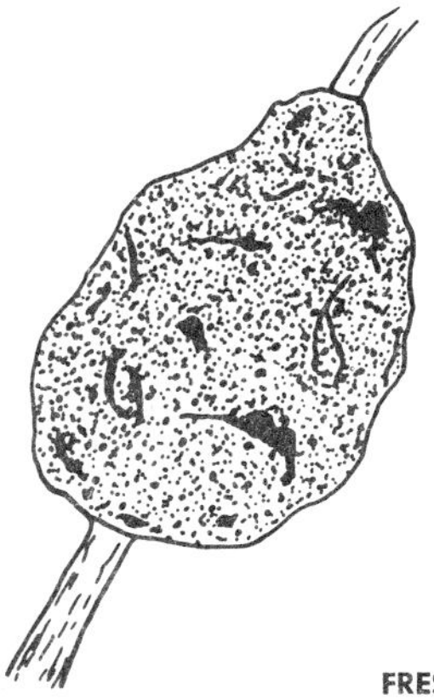

Figure 127
FRESHWATER SPONGE

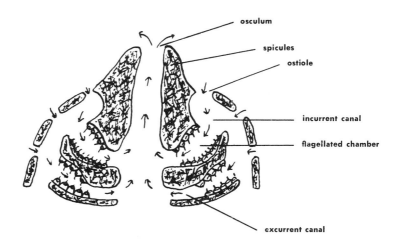

osculum

spicules

ostiole

incurrent canal

flagellated chamber

excurrent canal

Figure 128
DIAGRAM OF SECTION OF
FRESHWATER SPONGE

Figure 129
SPONGE SPICULE

by briskly waving flagella located in the chambers (flagellated chambers). It carries food to the cells that compose the sponge and also picks up waste products.

The soft tissues of the animal are supported on a latticelike framework or skeleton that is composed of small, transparent needles of silica. The needles, called spicules (Figure 129), the largest of which measure about one-hundredth of an inch, vary considerably in form and may be straight or curved, smooth or covered with brierlike points or dumbbell-shaped and sculptured, but they are always hooked or bound together in interlacing chains. A sponge may have spicules of several shapes, but the spicules are fairly constant for

154

any particular species and thus serve as a means of identification.

Although sponges are not readily seen, they occur in abundance in lakes, ponds, pools, and in clear, slow-flowing streams. Sponges are not free-swimming and are always sessile on a solid support: water-soaked logs, the leaves of submerged plants, and the undersides of stones. Some species branch out in slender, fingerlike processes and are suggestive of plants in form as well as in color; others may cloak submerged twigs in spindle-shaped masses or spread over stones in mats ten to fifteen inches across and an inch or more thick at the center. Frequently they live where they receive a considerable amount of sunlight and are then colored green by small one-celled plants that live within them. Sponges that live in the shade are of a pale color.

The commoner species of our freshwater sponges are the encrusting species that occur on the surfaces of submerged logs. Turn over one of these logs and you will likely find young sponges, showing as little circular fleshy yellow discs. These logs may also have green sponge colonies on the upper surface.

Transfer a freshwater sponge to a dish of water, add some India ink or a dye such as carmine, and you should be able to follow the flow of water in and out of the sponge. A

Figure 130
GEMMULES IN WINTER, HELD
AMONG SPICULES

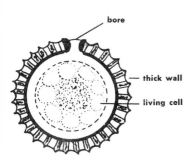

bore

thick wall

living cell

Figure 131
SECTION OF GEMMULE

hand lens may help you to observe this.

In the spring sponge colonies start from small asexual units called gemmules. These gemmules survive drying and freezing and carry the sponges over the winter season or periods of drought. Once a colony has made its appearance as a tiny fleck of white on a submerged stone or twig, it gradually increases in size, reaching its maximum growth in July and August. In early fall it usually begins to shrivel and by October and November is dead. Meanwhile, gemmules, or winter buds, have developed. These gemmules, held among the interlocked spicules (Figure 130), are the only parts of the sponge colony to live through the winter. They are little masses of living cells contained within a tough, hard, and highly resistant shell or outer coat. The outer coat has a pore through which the living cells can find their way out in the spring (Figure 131).

A study of these gemmules can be made very easily and with a minimum of equipment. In early winter look for the shriveled remains of a sponge colony. Clustered among the spicules, the gemmules resemble fig seeds and may be scraped into a jar of pond water and taken home. Place a few pieces of clean glass on the bottom of a pie plate and add some of the water from the jar. Set the pie

156

plate where it will not be jarred and will be out of direct sunlight, and finally drop two or three gemmules onto the glass. Leave them undisturbed for two or three days at room temperature, perhaps adding a little fresh water now and then, but if you do so be sure the gemmules are not shaken. Within a day or two they should stick to the glass. This attachment to the glass is the first sign of growth or that the soft sponge cells have grown out through the little hole in the gemmule shell onto the glass. You will notice a white plug in the hole and white drift around the dark gemmule. After three or four days of growth you will observe that little elevations have appeared on the surface. The tips are translucent bulbs at first, but they soon break through and the entire structure becomes chimneylike, with an open osculum at the top (Figure 132). If you now add a little India ink or carmine dye to the water as before, you will see through a hand lens the particles carried into the ostioles and out through the osculum. Remove the glass base with its colony from the water and hold it up to a light and you will see translucent spots and streaks. These indicate where canals and chambers have begun to form. When the colony is five or six days old you will be able to see the spicules.

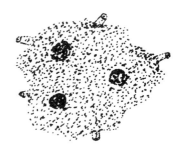

Figure 132
YOUNG SPONGE COLONY WITH GEMMULES FROM WHICH IT HAS DEVELOPED. NOTE CHIMNEYLIKE ELEVATIONS.

157

*We Inspect Some
Examples of
Insect Architecture*

THAT INSECTS are able to build shelters, some of which are cleverly constructed, is always a source of wonder. Indeed, many of them are capable builders, as the caddisworms.

The caddisworms are not worms but the larvae of small, mothlike insects, the caddis flies. Most of the caddisworms are caterpillar-like, and most of them construct portable cases in which they live and which they drag about wherever they go, with only the front end of the body and their legs projecting from the case as they travel. The cases of different species differ greatly in form and in materials used, but what is most interesting is that each species uses a specific kind of material and builds its own style of house. Particles of dead leaves, sticks, pebbles, sand, and other substances are used and cemented together with a silk secreted by modified salivary glands. The silk is not spun into a thread but is poured forth in a gluelike sheet upon the materials to be cemented together.

Caddisworms inhabit practically every kind of aquatic situation and can be found throughout the summer; a few species, especially the net builders, can be found all winter. The commoner caddisworms occur in almost every brook, where they may be seen creeping over the bottom. They look much like moving sticks and are sometimes called stick worms.

A caddisworm differs from a caterpillar in that it has only one pair of prolegs, the anal prolegs. The mouthparts are fitted for chewing and the thoracic legs are well developed. In the case-building species three tubercles are present on the first abdominal segment, one dorsal and one on each side (Figure 133). These tubercles are known as "spacing humps" and provide a space between the insect and its case so that water for respiration may circulate freely. Some species, however, do not have these tubercles. Caddisworms extract the oxygen from the water by means of filamentous gills. In many species they are attached along the sides of the abdomen and are completely protected by the case. The water is made to circulate over the gills by undulating movements of the body. How does the caddisworm manage to hold on to its case as it moves about? The prolegs are

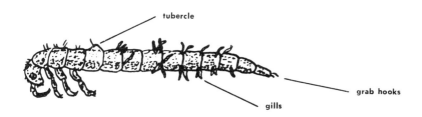

Figure 133
CADDISWORM

159

provided with hooks. Called drag hooks, they anchor the caddisworm to its case.

When caddisworms outgrow their cases, they either discard the old case and build a new one or enlarge the present one by building onto the front end. When full grown and ready to pupate, some species cement a stone or grains of sand over the front opening, others build a silken lid with a slit in it, and still others fashion a silken grating in each end. The purpose is to prevent intruders from entering the case during the pupal period, but at no time is the opening completely closed so as to exclude water, so necessary for respiration; water can still flow in and out and circulate over the gills.

The pupae of the caddis flies are as aquatic as the larvae and like them have gills. They are active and like the larvae continue their undulating motion to keep the water flowing over the gills. The pupae of species that live in swift water, when ready to emerge as adults, leave their cases, swim to the surface, shed their pupal skin, and fly into the air. The pupae of species that inhabit quiet waters climb out on the shore or upon projecting stones, and there transform.

Figure 134 shows a case made of rectangular bits of thin leaves arranged in rings. It measures about an inch long and is made by the caddisworm, Neuronia, found in ponds and gently flowing streams. Figure 135 shows a case made with narrow strips of leaves arranged spirally and securely glued together. The maker, Phryganea, occurs in ponds among submerged plants. A case made of sand grains is shown in Figure 136. The larva, Molanna, lives on the sandy bottoms of slow streams and ponds. Figure 137 illustrates a cornucopia-shaped case made of sand grains. Leptocerus, which occupies it, lives in the riffles of stony brooks. A case composed of sticks or of pieces of grass placed crosswise forming a case known as the log cabin type is depicted in Figure 138. Its maker, Limmophilus, inhabits ponds and slow-moving streams. So does a species that makes its case of the shells of water snails. Helicopsyche, a caddisworm of stony streams,

Figure 134
CASE OF NEURONIA

Figure 135
CASE OF PHRYGANEA

Figure 136
CASE OF MOLANNA

Figure 137
CASE OF LEPTOCERUS

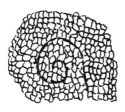

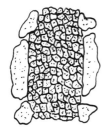

makes a case of sand grains that looks so much like the shell of a snail that it has been mistaken for a mollusk (Figure 139). Another case, also made of sand grains (Figure 140), has stones glued to each side to serve as ballast. Its tenant, Goera, dwells in riffles of swift streams, and the stones prevent the case from being carried away by the current. A most remarkable case is one made of minute twigs, root fibers, and fragments of wood cut to the proper length to form even, straight edges. The case diverges toward the anterior end. During the first weeks of its existence the maker, Brachycentrus, lives in the side waters of brooks, where it forages along the banks. Then it moves into the center of the stream and attaches one front edge of the larger end to a submerged rock or stone. Securely cemented to its support, the insect now lives a sedentary life. It always selects an exposed situation and faces up-current in a position shown in Figure 141, with its head projecting slightly and its legs extended upstream. In this position it is able to grasp and devour small larvae and bits of vegetation that float within its reach. Another species, Glossosoma, makes a turtle-shaped case of small stones (Figure 142). It is found on brook bottoms.

Not all caddisworms build portable cases; some species (Polycentropus) occupy tubes

162

made of silk and debris that are attached permanently to a support, as a rock. These species, which live in waterfalls, riffles, and rapid streams, are of particular interest since they spin silken nets to capture food. The nets are spun adjacent to the tubes in which the insects live, are funnel-shaped (Figure 143), and at the downstream end have an opening with a strainer. Sometimes the nets of Hydropsyche are spun in crevices between stones, but usually they are built up from a flat surface and then take the form of semi-elliptical cups kept distended by the flowing water (Figure 144). Food materials, such as algae, insect larvae, and various small animals that pass through the net are trapped by the strainer.

The caddisworms that live in ponds and quiet waters, mainly those that make portable cases, do well in an aquarium, an enameled pan, or a photographic developing tray. Most of these species live on vegetable matter, and when collected some of the plant life, usually algae found growing in the same habitat, should also be taken to provide food. Also provide them with the same materials used in building their cases. To observe caddisworms at their building activities, remove them from their cases; they will immediately begin to build new ones, if building materials are

163

Figure 141
CASE OF BRACHYCENTRUS

Figure 142
CASE OF GLOSSOSOMA

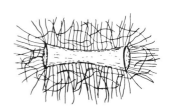

Figure 143
NEST OF POLYCENTROPUS

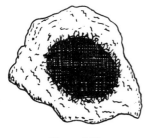

available. Should you wonder what a caddis-worm would do if dispossessed of its home and deprived of its normal building materials, there is one way to find out. Substitute other materials and see what happens.

ADVENTURE 34

We Test the Behavior of the Crayfish

THE CRAYISH, or crawfish, as it is known in some parts of the country, is a familiar animal to every boy and girl studying biology in high school. Unfortunately most of them know it as a pickled specimen to be dissected; few have seen it in its natural habitat. Yet it is a common inhabitant of ponds and streams, where it may be seen by day hiding under a flat stone or in a burrow in the bankside. The crayfish, which looks and behaves much like a miniature lobster (Figure 145) is most active at night. When darkness begins to set in, it comes out of its hiding place and crawls around in search of food. At other times it remains concealed, its antennae extended out in the water to detect the approach of a fish, water insect, or other animal that it eagerly grasps should the hapless victim come within reach of its large pincer claws. The crayfish is carnivorous to a high degree, but it also eats all kinds of dead plant and animal matter.

How the crayfish feeds can be observed in

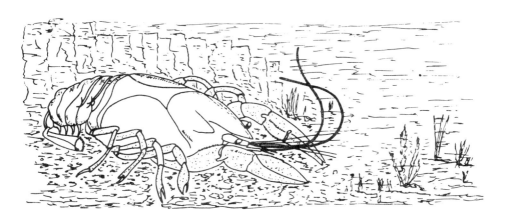

Figure 145
CRAYFISH

an aquarium by offering the animal a little fresh meat. It makes a novel aquarium pet and can be the subject of many interesting observations. An aquarium with some mud on the bottom, a few water plants, and a flat stone for it to hide beneath will provide an ideal home, but a large enameled pan with about two inches of water and with sides sufficiently high so that it cannot climb out will serve. One crayfish to an aquarium should be the rule, for when several are kept together they are apt to fight, with the possible loss of a limb or the death of one or all.

Although .the crayfish is capable of swimming, it moves about principally by walking on its fourth pair of legs. The second and

165

third pairs are little used for this purpose, being modified as grasping organs and cleaning tools, while the fifth pair acts chiefly as props and to push the animal forward. Note that it can move in any direction. The crayfish rarely swims and then only under duress, as when frightened or shocked. At such times it extends its abdomen, spreads out the uropods and telson, then by contractions of the abdominal muscles bends the abdomen and darts backward. From experiments and observations it appears that swimming is not a voluntary but a reflex act.

It may surprise you to learn that a crayfish, whether at rest or in motion, is always in a state of unstable equilibrium. Gravity tends to pull it over on its side, but, to counteract this tendency, the crayfish has organs of equilibrium, or balancing organs, as they are sometimes referred to. These organs or structures, called statocysts, are located in the basal segment of each antennule, the shorter of the two pairs of antennae. They are chitin-lined sacs with a ridge with many fine sensory hairs that are excited or stimulated by a single nerve fiber. The crayfish places small grains of sand, called statoliths, among these hairs, remaining attached to them by a cementing substance secreted by certain glands. Contact of the statoliths with the sensory hairs provides the stimulus that enables the animal to maintain a normal position. During the time of molting (a crayfish changes its skin periodically to allow for an increase in size during growth) the crayfish has temporarily lost its power of orientation, since the statocysts are also shed. It does not regain its sense of equilibrium until it has replaced the lost grains of sand.

Place a crayfish on its back and you will find that it has considerable difficulty righting itself. Usually it regains its normal position by raising itself on one side and then falling over. Another method sometimes used is to contract the flexor abdominal muscles. By so doing a quick backward flop results in bringing the animal right side up.

Sense organs of touch, located in specialized hairlike bristles, or setae, are found on various parts of the body but are more abundant on the mouthparts, pincers, and telson. The animal exhibits a positive reaction to touch and always seeks to keep its body in contact with a solid object. When at rest the crayfish always tries to keep one side of its back in contact with the walls of its retreat, a position that is undoubtedly of advantage, as it places the animal in a position of safety.

Since the animal prefers to remain hidden by day and ventures out at dusk, it seems rather obvious that it must show a negative response to light. Shine a light on a crayfish and it immediately retreats. Cover a flashlight with different pieces of colored paper and you will find that it prefers colored lights to white light. This negative response to light is also of advantage, as it prompts the animal to seek a dark place where it is hidden from enemies.

The animal also shows definite responses to chemical stimuli. Add a little acid or a pinch of salt or sugar to the water and it responds negatively by a scratching, rubbing, or pulling action depending on the part of the body affected. Reactions to food are in part due to a chemical sense and are positive. Place a little meat juice in the water near the crayfish and it responds by moving its antennae slightly and its mouthparts vigorously, that is, they perform rapid chewing movements. Though the meat juice makes the animal generally restless and makes it move toward the source of the stimulus, it appears to depend chiefly on touch to locate its food.

Crayfishes are able to form habits and to modify them under changing conditions. Here is an interesting field for investigation, and no doubt you will want to conduct experiments. You will find that the animals learn by experience and that they modify their behavior slowly or quickly, depending on how familiar they are with any given situation.

WHEN WE SPEAK of fleas we immediately think of the insects that even with the best of care sometimes get on our pet dog or cat. We are not likely to associate these insects with ponds and streams, and rightly so, for fleas are not adapted to live in such an environment. But there are animals called water fleas that do live there. Actually they are not fleas or even insects, but crustaceans.

Most of the water fleas, known scientifically as cladocerans, are small, even microscopic, although a few, such as the beautiful and fierce carnivore Leptodora (Figure 146), may measure about three-quarters of an inch in length. Most of them have the body but not the head enclosed in a transparent shell, or carapace. The shell is thin, finely reticulated, striated, or sculptured and in some species with conspicuous spines, and so transparent that the internal structures can be clearly seen with a microscope. They have long been favorite animals for study.

Water fleas use the second pair of antennae for swimming. In Daphnia (Figure 147),

ADVENTURE 35

We Are Intrigued by the Water Fleas

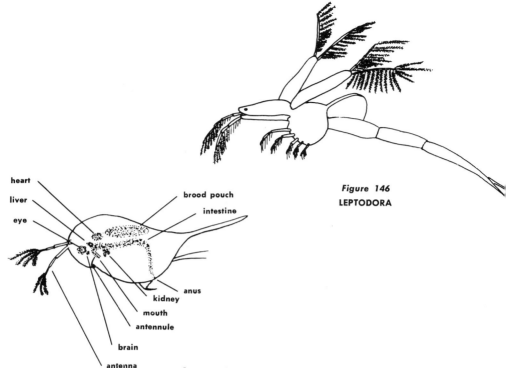

Figure 146
LEPTODORA

heart
liver
eye
brood pouch
intestine
anus
kidney
mouth
antennule
brain
antenna

Figure 147
DAPHNIA

Figure 148
CHYDORUS

where the antennae are larger and well developed, the strokes are short, quick, uneven and swimming is accomplished by a series of jumps, but in species where the antennae are shorter, as in Chydorus (Figure 148), the strokes are longer, more smoothly made, and swimming is steadier. Examine a water flea closely. It has five pairs of leaf-shaped legs. The legs move rapidly and create currents of water. These pass over the respiratory valves at the bases of the legs and also carry particles of food to the mouth.

Water fleas occur in all kinds of fresh-

170

waters, but the greatest variety of species is found in quiet, shallow waters overgrown with waterweeds. The animals forage on the waterweeds and subsist on bacteria, the lesser green algae, diatoms, and minute particles of organic matter. Some species dwell on the bottom, where they scramble over the mud. These are little given to swimming. A few species swim in half-open waters between floating leaves. Water fleas are abundant in open water, where they feed on floating diatoms and algae of the plankton and constitute a large part of the plankton society. They are abundant during the summer season, feeding close to the surface of the water at night and by day dropping to a lower level. Large numbers of water fleas can be seen near the shore, and thousands of them can be gathered by dipping a pan in the water. A plankton-towing net or throw net may also be used* (Figure 149). For some reason the population of

* The net is thrown from the shore and then pulled back through the water.

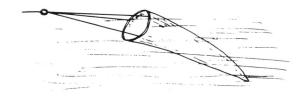

Figure 149
**PLANKTON-TOWING NET FOR
SKIMMING THE SURFACE**

cladocerans is variable. For instance, they may swarm in untold numbers at some favored spot, while a short distance away only a few or none at all can be found. Again they may swarm in a given spot on one day and on the following have disappeared.

Not only can their internal organs be seen clearly with a microscope, but also metabolic processes such as digestion. If you have a microscope or have access to one, collect different species and study them. Daphnia is one of the commoner and can usually be found any time of the year, though it is more abundant in the spring and fall. Watch the path of food through the digestive tract, then the rapidly beating heart, which is located in the dorsal region behind the eyes. You can change the rate of the heartbeat by warming the slide or by adding a trace of adrenalin (about 0.01 per cent). Since the heartbeat is normally fast, you may not be able to detect any increase easily. Also study the circulation, the respiratory system, and note peristalsis. Since Daphnia and other water fleas are active little animals and may not remain quiet enough for you to examine them properly, you can slow them down by anesthetizing them. For this purpose a life slide should be used. This is a microscope slide with a depression. Fill the depression with a solution of two parts of 1 per cent Chloretone and five parts of water and place the animal in it.

Water fleas are a staple diet of young fishes, but their importance is not their size but their enormous reproductive capacity. During the summer season broods of eggs are produced in the brood pouches of the females every two or three days. The young develop rapidly and soon produce eggs. A female Daphnia is capable of producing as many as thirteen billion progeny in sixty days. In common with many other water fleas Daphnia has two kinds of eggs: thin-shelled eggs, produced during the summer, and thick-shelled eggs, produced in autumn. The summer eggs, which develop without fertilization, hatch only into female Daphnia, so that one female generation follows another. On the approach of cold weather, a decline in food supply, and other unfavorable conditions, the series of female generations ends. Some of the females now produce eggs that develop into males. Mating takes place and fertilized eggs are produced. These resting eggs are relatively large compared to the summer eggs, contain more yolk, and have thick, horny shells. They are enclosed in a saddlelike shell, called the ephippium, which consists of two pieces shaped like watch crystals, with their edges fitted closely together. Figure 150 shows a

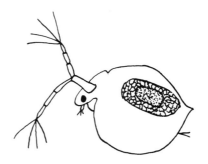

Figure 150
CERIODAPHNIA WITH
EPHIPPIUM

species of water flea, Ceriodaphnia, with an
ephippium. Protected in such a manner, the
eggs are carried through the winter and in
the spring develop into females that begin a
new cycle. The terms "summer eggs" and
"winter eggs" are somewhat misleading, for
species of water fleas that regularly produce
resting eggs in the fall will also produce them
in summer under certain conditions, while
there are some species that regularly produce
resting eggs in the summer.

Since water fleas serve as food for young
fishes as well as other freshwater animals such
as hydra and spotted newts, they are frequently cultured, so a supply of them may
always be at hand. A great many methods

have been developed for maintaining water fleas, especially Daphnia, which seems to be the most popular of these animals. Should you want to keep a stock of Daphnia on hand for your aquarium inhabitants, one of the most successful methods is to fill a large battery jar with tap water and let it stand overnight to allow any harmful gases to escape. The battery jar is next placed in strong sunlight and inoculated with one-celled or non-filamentous algae from a "soupy green" aquarium. The "green water" is left standing for two or three days and the Daphnia are then added, together with a small amount of hard-boiled egg yolk mashed into a paste with a little of the "green water." A suspension of yeast to stimulate growth can also be added. To make a yeast suspension, cut up small pieces of a yeast cake and place them in a flask or bottle containing some water. Shake the flask or bottle vigorously until a suspension forms. Add the suspension to the culture medium until the water is slightly milky. When the water fleas have cleared it, add the same amount again. The water should be completely changed once a month and left at a temperature of between 12° C. and 24° C. Aeration is not necessary, but stirring the water once a day might be advisable to maintain a satisfactory culture.

We Come upon the Unexpected

FROM SPRING and throughout the summer months into late fall caterpillars are almost everywhere, feeding on the leaves of woodland trees, the shrubs along the roadside, and on our garden plants. We associate caterpillars with plants and therefore with a terrestrial habitat; it seems inconceivable that they would live in water. Yet there are a few species that do.

One of these caterpillars, *Nymphula maculalis,* lives on water lilies that grow in quiet waters. Rather, it lives in a case that it makes by biting off two pieces of lily pad, fastening the edges of the two together with strands of silk, shiny side out, and attaching the case to the lower surface of the same lily pad (Figure 151). The case serves the caterpillar not only as a shelter but also as a source of food, for the insect first feeds on the inner layer of the walls and later when it is older on the outside shiny layer.

Since the case is below the surface and filled with water, how does the caterpillar breathe, since caterpillars are normally terrestrial insects and air breathers? Like other aquatic insects that are not air breathers, the caterpillars take in oxygen by means of bushy, branched gills that extend from the sides of the body. However, a related species, *Nymphula obliteralis,* that also lives in a case

Figure 151
LILY-LEAF CATERPILLAR AND CASE, *NYMPHULA MUCALALIS*

176

Figure 152
CASE OF *NYMPHULA
OBLITERALIS*

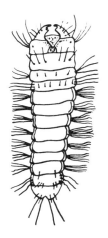

Figure 153
CATERPILLAR OF ELOPHILA

beneath the surface (Figure 152) does not
have gills. For its oxygen this caterpillar de-
pends on a bubble of air that surrounds it in
its leaf case. Both these lily-leaf caterpillars,
as they are known, pupate within their cases
and transform into moths.

It doesn't seem too strange that caterpillars
should take to an aquatic habitat, since insects are able to adapt themselves to all sorts
of environmental conditions, but we would
hardly expect them to seek the haunts of
mayflies and stone-flies. And yet a caterpillar,
Elophila fulicalis (Figure 153), is found in
the turbulent waters of a rushing stream.
Here it lives beneath a silken canopy that it

177

weaves and attaches to the water-washed rocks, breathing oxygen through gills and feeding on the algal ooze growing on the rocks. Look for the silken canopy and note how it is designed to permit water to circulate freely within it. When it is time to transform, the caterpillar makes a pupal case and suspends it by silken threads to the top of the canopy. In June and July newly emerged moths may be seen swarming about the vegetation along the banks of the stream.

ADVENTURE 37

We Are Introduced to an Efficiency Expert

At a casual glance leeches (Figures 154 to 156) may not have much appeal, yet they are not without a certain beauty, since many of them are beautifully colored with soft green, brown, and yellow tints. Of more interest they represent a high degree of efficiency in their mode of living. Since leeches are easy to keep in an aquarium or merely a jar of water, providing the water is changed daily, and require a feeding only every few weeks, they make apt subjects for study and investigation.

Leeches can be easily collected. They abound in ponds and sluggish ditches, where they lurk under stones and logs, on water plants, or attached to various animals, and

Figure 155
BROOK LEECH

Figure 154
TURTLE LEECH, VENTRAL
SURFACE, SHOWING SUCKERS

Figure 156
COMMON BLOODSUCKER

on the bottom mud; a few live on stones and boards in swift streams, but for the most part they prefer quiet waters. One way to collect them is to examine boards and stones, and if they are found attached the animals can be removed by sliding a knife under them and dropping them into a collecting bottle. Another method is to wade out into a pond and within a few minutes you will find them attached to your bare legs. If you are averse to this method, wear rubber boots; the leeches will attach themselves to the boots just as readily.

Various species differ in minor details but in general are much alike. They are segmented animals, with a body more or less depressed and narrowed toward the ends, more abruptly toward the posterior and tapering toward the anterior, which is necklike and extremely pliant. A distinct head is absent. If you want to know how a leech attaches itself to an object and tenaciously clings to it, look at the strong suckers at each end of the body. The particular adaptation that enables leeches to suck blood is the sucking mouth, or, more specifically, a "suction-bulb" pharynx (Figure 157) and triradiate toothed jaws that are absent, however, in some species. When a leech feeds, it selects a spot well supplied with blood vessels. As the toothed jaws enter the skin a small amount of the animal's saliva enters the wound. The saliva contains a substance called hirudin, which functions as an anticoagulant, or thinning agent, so that the blood can readily be sucked up.

The blood passes into the crop, which is of enormous size and can store considerable quantities of blood. As a matter of fact the leech can ingest three times its own weight in blood. The blood stored is the solid part because the fluid part is drawn off through the kidneys while the leech is in the process of sucking blood from the wound. Digestion is a slow process. It may take nine months or more for a full supply of blood to be com-

Figure 157
ANTERIOR SUCKER AND TRIRADIATE JAWS

180

pletely digested. This is why meals are few and far between.

Because some leeches suck blood they are called bloodsuckers. This is somewhat misleading, because all leeches do not live on blood. Some of them feed on worms, insect larvae; a few are scavengers of dead animals. Even those that are bloodsuckers are curiously varied in their eating habits. For instance, a leech may feed on snail meat one time and suck turtle or frog blood the next. As a group the leeches exhibit both parasitic and predatory habits; while some species are predatory others are permanent parasites. As a group, the leeches may be wavering on the brink of parasitism.

Leeches vary considerably in size, from the small pale species half an inch long to the large blackish horseleeches (Figure 158) a foot or more in length. The horseleeches live in the mud by the sides of pools, ditches, and streams, where they feed principally on aquatic worms and mollusks, but they are not averse to sucking blood from wading animals wherever they get the chance. When collecting leeches you will observe that many of them are marked with concealing colors and patterns that blend with the broken shadows of water-soaked leaves of their habitat and efficiently conceal them.

Figure 158
HORSELEECH

Leeches are extremely sensitive to light or shadows passing over them, to vibrations in the water, and even to slight changes in the flavor of the water. Pass your hand over the aquarium or jar so that a shadow falls on them. They immediately become quite excited and start swinging their heads about. Place your finger on the bottom of the aquarium or jar and they begin to move about. If they pass over your fingerprint they indicate they have detected its odor. Dissolve the slightest amount of any substance in the water and they react to it. Even the slightest disturbance in the water makes them restless and they at once attempt to discover the source of it.

In captivity leeches may be given small pieces of raw beef liver, chopped raw meat, earthworms, or snail meat. A meal should last them for several weeks. One precaution to observe is to cover the aquarium or jar with a piece of wire screening or cheesecloth; otherwise they may crawl away. If you are patient and lucky you may be successful in getting them to reproduce. Every leech has both male and female organs of reproduction, but even so the sperms of one must be transferred to the body of another for the eggs to fertilize. In their natural habitat leeches as a rule lay their eggs in spring and summer.

Many species deposit their eggs in minute pockets attached to stones, others within a horny cocoon that may be dropped in the mud or attached to plants, rocks, and debris, and still others carry their eggs in a capsule beneath the body and the young are brooded there for a time after hatching (Figure 159). In the aquarium they may be glued to any upright support or merely dropped on the bottom.

Figure 159
LEECH CARRYING YOUNG

ADVENTURE 38

We Discover an Incongruity

WE THINK of spiders as being land animals. They do not appear adapted to an aquatic environment any more than the caterpillars, yet several species are capable of running over the surface of the water and even diving when necessary. One of them is so adroit at this that it is known as the diving dolomedes.

The diving dolomedes is a fairly large spider and may often be seen on or near water. Look for it when you visit a pond in the summer and observe how easily it runs over the surface of the water. The female has a yellow median band on the basal half of the abdomen, and on each side of this yellow line at the base of the abdomen there is a narrow yellow line. Between these lines and the tip of the abdomen there are from

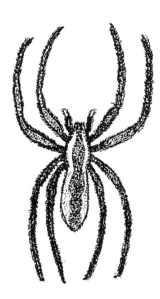

Figure 160
SIX-DOTTED DOLOMEDES

Figure 161
STERNUM OF DOLOMEDES

three to six pairs of small white and yellow spots, each pair being connected by a slightly recurved black line. The male is quite different in appearance and may be recognized by the black narrow margin of the cephalothorax and a broad yellowish band within the margin.

The diving dolomedes often preys on large aquatic insects and dives when alarmed. At such times it carries down with it bubbles of air and can remain submerged fairly long. There are several species of dolomedes found near water, and all can run on the surface and dive. The six-spotted dolomedes (Figure 160) was once observed diving and capturing a small fish. The spider held on with a deadly grip until the fish became exhausted, whereupon the spider dragged it from the water. The six-spotted dolomedes is beautiful and is easily recognized because of its color and its size, measuring from three-fifths to four-fifths of an inch in length. It is dark greenish gray in color, with a white band on each side extending the entire length of the body. There are two rows of white spots on the surface of the abdomen and six dark dots on the sternum (Figure 161), which is the ventral wall of the thorax and which occupies the entire space between the two rows of legs. The six dots suggested the name.

OF ALL THE inhabitants of our freshwaters none are more entertaining to watch than the scuds, or amphipods. They are small crustaceans shaped like fleas, with an arched back, a narrow body, and flattened sides. The legs on the thorax are adapted for climbing, and the abdominal appendages for swimming and jumping, all of which they can do with facility.

Although they can be seen with the naked eye, they are too small to watch in their native habitat and can better be observed in an aquarium planted with water plants as Elodea, Nitella or Myriophyllum, which can be obtained from almost any pond, and containing a few dead leaves. Here at close range we can watch them swim, climb, jump, and perform acrobatic stunts among the water plants. They can be collected with a dip net, pan, or by holding a wide-mouth bottle in the water and letting it flow in. They are active throughout the year and can be collected beneath the ice in winter.

Two common amphipods in our ponds and streams are Gammarus (Figure 162) and Hyalella (Figure 163). Gammarus is an excellent swimmer but seems to prefer the sheltering crevices of dense foliage rather than open water. Watching it leap and dodge in the aquarium reminds us of the rabbit.

We Are Captivated by the Antics of the Scuds

185

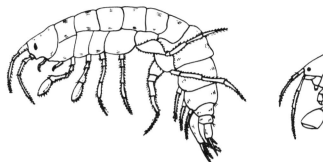

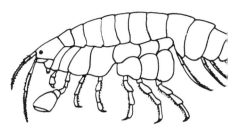

Figure 162
GAMMARUS

Figure 163
HYALELLA

Hyalella and Gammarus gather in early
spring in mats of Spirogyra, where they feed
on the dead filaments. This is a good time
to collect them. Both of them, like all amphipods, are herbivores and feed on a great
variety of both living and dead plant life.
They have also been seen feeding on snails,
tadpoles, and other small animals. Numerous
Hyalellas were once observed feeding on the
decomposing flesh of a dead water bird.

Both Hyalella and Gammarus will mate in
the aquarium. The male clasps the female
with his grasping legs and swims about holding her beneath him for a period of several
days. These amphipods are of especial interest because, unlike other crustaceans, they
lack a larval life. The female carries the fer-

186

tilized eggs in a brood pouch beneath the thorax, and here the eggs hatch in from nine to thirty days as miniature adults quite capable of fending for themselves. The scuds are not as prolific as some other aquatic herbivores, but one pair of Hyalellas has been known to produce a clutch of some dozen and a half eggs fifteen times in one hundred fifty-two days. Frequently a female may carry a previous brood of young in her brood pouch during the mating swim.

FOR MUCH the same reason that the lions and tigers of the jungle appeal to our imagination, the diving beetles (Figure 164) of our ponds and streams have a similar fascination. They are probably the fiercest and most predatory of all water insects, preying greedily on other aquatic insects, tadpoles, snails, and small fishes. And yet, to find one of these beetles hanging in an upside-down position from the surface of a quiet pool, we get the impression that no insect could be more agreeable or friendly to the other inhabitants.

Diving beetles are usually brown or black and range in size from only a few hundredths of an inch to more than an inch and a half in length. Many of the lesser forms are flecked

ADVENTURE 40

We Hunt the Water Tigers

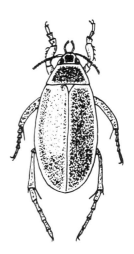

Figure 164
DIVING BEETLE, DYTISCUS

and streaked with yellow. Sometimes they are confused with the water scavenger beetles. Their antennae, however, are slender and threadlike, whereas those of the scavenger beetles are club-shaped. In some species of diving beetles the males have cuplike suckers on the front feet which function as clinging organs and are used to clasp the female when mating. Like most water beetles they have flattened hind legs used effectively in swimming. Before they dive they raise their wing covers to form a reservoir for air that they breathe when submerged. The amount of air taken in this manner permits them to remain below the surface for fairly long periods. When the air is exhausted or has become impure, the beetles rise to the surface, force out the old air, and take in a fresh supply. The females of some species show a dimorphism in that some have furrowed elytra, or wing covers, while others have smooth ones.

Diving beetles are common in ponds and pools and should be looked for among the vegetation in the shallows and near the shore where they forage for food. They can be collected by sweeping the water with a net.

The larvae, known as water tigers because of their bloodthirsty habits, are elongate, spindle-shaped, with a large oval, rounded, or flattened head (Figure 165). Their large,

Figure 165
WATER TIGER CAPTURING
TADPOLE

sickle-shaped, hollow jaws are admirably fitted for grasping prey and sucking the body juices of their victims, as a canal leads from an opening at the tip to the mouth. If you want to watch how a water tiger catches its prey, place one in an aquarium. Drop some other kind of aquatic insect into the water. The moment the water tiger catches sight of a prospective meal, it becomes alert, extends its jaws, and when its victim comes within reach, lunges forward and seizes it.

Water tigers have six well-developed legs, which they use in swimming. Some species have a pair of spiracles at the tip of the abdomen and project them into the air at intervals in order to breathe; others have tracheal gills that trail from the sides of the body. Since these forms are not dependent on air, they are generally found prowling along the bottom of the pond or pool.

Both the larvae and adults of the diving beetles do well in an aquarium if well supplied with live food, although an adult was once kept in a vessel of water for three and a half years on raw meat. During the winter they will take mealworms, which can be purchased at a pet store. They have also been kept alive for some months on prepared fish food consisting of a mixture of cereal, powdered shrimp, and ground ant eggs.

190

WE USUALLY give little thought to tadpoles, for one tadpole seems much like another. But they are not all alike. Tadpoles of one species differ from those of another as much as the adult frogs themselves. Even the eggs differ. For instance, the eggs of the spring peeper are white or creamy and black or brownish, the eggs of the common tree frog are brown and cream or yellow, the eggs of the leopard frog are black and white, and those of the pickerel frog are brown and bright yellow. They even vary in size. Surprisingly, the eggs of some of the smaller species, such as the robber frogs and little chorus frogs, are the largest, while the smallest are those of the large bullfrog. The eggs of some of our common species of frogs and toads are shown in Figures 166 to 171.

Unlike the frog tadpoles, those of the toads are small and very dark or blackish. The tadpole of our common toad is very dark, almost black, and measures one and a half inches when full grown. It has an ovoid body, broader at the vent or anus than at the eyes, with a low dorsal tail crest extending slightly onto the body, and a short tail having a rounded tip. Contrast this tadpole with that of the wood frog and see how much they can differ. The tadpole of the wood frog is a deep olive about two inches long, with a dorsal

We Engange in a
Matter of
Identification

191

Figure 167
EGG OF LEOPARD FROG

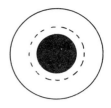

Figure 168
EGG OF WOOD FROG

Figure 169
EGG OF GREEN FROG

Figure 170
EGG OF COMMON TREE FROG

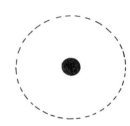

Figure 171
EGG OF BULLFROG

crest and a long tail having a tapering tip. Now consider the tadpole of the common tree frog. It has a long scarlet or orange-vermilion tail, with black blotches around the edges of the crest, and a long tip. It measures from one and three-fifths to two inches in length. Even smaller, the tadpole of the spring peeper is only an inch long. It is delicate-appearing, with the undersurface of the body a reddish bronze shining with a metallic luster.

192

Much larger than either of these two frog tadpoles, that of the leopard frog reaches a length of three and one-eighth inches. It has a tail lighter than the body, and translucent crests marked with fine spots and pencilings. The tadpole of the pickerel frog is about the same size but greenish in color with a creamy belly. Both the body and tail are covered with fine black dots and the crests are black and very clouded. The tadpole of the green frog is olive green and not quite as large, measuring only two and nine-sixteenths inches. The elongate tail with an acute tip is green mottled with brown. The largest of all is the bullfrog tadpole. It is from four to six and three-fifths inches in length and brown with fine specklings of black. Tadpoles found in late summer and early fall are either those of the green frog or bullfrog, since the green frog takes one year and the bullfrog two or more years to transform.

In learning how to identify tadpoles we can do so in two ways: we can collect the eggs and hatch them as described in Adventure 11; we can capture the tadpoles directly with a water net.

Some interesting experiments can be conducted with tadpoles by giving them thyroxine tablets. Thyroxine is a hormone that stimulates the metamorphosis of tadpoles, and by using various amounts you can determine the rate at which metamorphosis can be accelerated. Crush and dissolve five two-grain thyroxine tablets in five cc. of distilled water. Weigh out an equal amount of whole-wheat flour and mix the flour with the tablets. Spread the paste in a thin layer on a piece of glass and leave to dry. When dry, powder the mixture and store in a closed bottle in a refrigerator.

Next place several tadpoles in separate glass dishes filled with pond water. Set one aside as a control. Using different concentrations of the powdered mixture (a small scale for weighing the amounts is essential), add the powdered mixture to the separate dishes daily, making sure that you add the same concentration each day to specified dishes, which should be labeled to avoid error. In other words, Dish A should receive a specified concentration, Dish B a specified concentration, and so on. The control dish, of course, should not receive any of the powdered mixture. About 50 mg. of the powder per tadpole is a suggested amount. Continue the experiment for about a week and determine what effect various concentrations have on metamorphosis. Feed the tadpoles parboiled spinach or lettuce and change the water each day to prevent fouling. Be sure to keep a record of all observations. Note, for instance, time of appearance of hind and fore limbs, changes in the length of tail and in the shape of the head and body, and length of time to complete transformation.

Instead of using thyroxine you may want to try iodine, which is the main fraction of thyroxine. Dissolve 0.1 gram of iodine crystals in 5 cc. of a 95 per cent solution of alcohol. Dilute this to 1 liter with distilled water. This is a stock solution of a concentration of 1:10,000. Weaker solutions may be made by adding more water.

ADVENTURE 42

We Quest for the One-eyed Cyclops

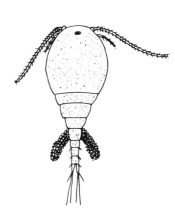

Figure 172
CYCLOPS

LOCATE a ditch filled or partly filled with water, immerse an empty bottle in it, allow the water to run in, then hold the bottle up to the light. If you see small white specks moving jerkily about you have collected some water hoppers, likely Cyclops (Figure 172), one of the commoner of these small animals.

The water hoppers, or copepods, as they are known scientifically, are all small and more or less pear-shaped, with a body tapering to a forked tail, a pair of long antennae, and four pairs of thoracic swimming legs. The antennae are primarily sense organs but are often used in locomotion and in some

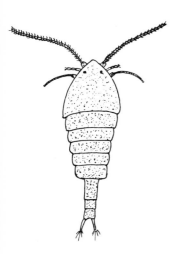

Figure 173
DIAPTOMUS

males for clasping the female. Water hoppers are perennial inhabitants of ponds, pools, and open waters and feed on microscopic organisms and any kind of decayed matter, but they prefer decomposing plant tissue. Water hoppers that live among the plankton on the surface of open water are likely to be transparent and slender, whereas those that live in the weeds or near the shore are shorter and often dark-colored. Some species of Diaptomus (Figure 173) are red, blue, or purple and when they occur in large numbers color the water. Water hoppers are of considerable economic importance, for they, as well as the fairy shrimps, water fleas, and ostracods, provide the necessary link between the small organic plant organisms, the inorganic constituents of the water, and the higher animals for which they serve as food, especially young fishes.

Water hoppers may be seen with the naked eye but are best viewed with a hand lens or a microscope. One of the commoner is Cyclops (Figure 172), so named after the mythological one-eyed giant because it has a single eye in the middle of its head. Since Cyclops and other copepods are active little animals and will not remain in one place long enough to observe with a microscope, follow the procedure as suggested in Adventure 35.

196

Females are often collected and may be recognized by the pair of egg pockets hanging from their sides. When mating the male Cyclops clasps the female with his antennae and together they swim about. While swimming, the sperms, in sufficient numbers to fertilize several clutches of eggs, are transferred to the body of the female. Copepods produce two kinds of eggs: summer ones, which are produced often and develop quickly, and resting eggs, usually formed in seasons of cold and drought. Young copepods are quite unlike their parents in appearance. They are flat and oval and are called nauplii (Figure 174) (singular nauplius). Following a series of molts, they gradually acquire the typical copepod form. Copepods such as Cyclops do very well in an aquarium where they may be observed and studied or used as food for hydras and other freshwater animals. They can be fed on protozoa, which you can culture and so have a stock always on hand. One method of culturing protozoa is to prepare a hay infusion by steeping hay, preferably timothy, in hot water for an hour or more. Then strain the liquid through a piece of cloth or filter paper into an open dish. Let stand for a few days and then add some pond water. A rich culture of protozoa should develop within a week. As this culture will not

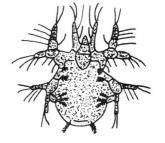

Figure 174
NAUPLIUS OF CYCLOPS

last indefinitely a fresh culture should be prepared every two or three weeks to be assured of a steady supply.

We Turn Our Attention to the Ostracods

THE OSTRACODS mentioned in the last adventure look like microscopic clams, since they have the head, body, and appendages enclosed within a bivalve shell. Figure 175 shows Cypris, a common ostracod. As with the clams the shells or valves swing on hinges and close by muscles. Unlike clams the ostracods do not move by a muscular foot, but by jointed appendages that they extend between the two shells and kick rapidly backward. They glide or jerk themselves over leaf surfaces and climb up plant stems with a surprising agility.

Although some ostracods are free-swimming, most of them are creeping animals that seem to prefer the sunny, protected parts of ponds. Here we should look for them. Since they are omnivorous scavengers, being especially partial to decayed vegetation, few of them occur in clear water. Hence many live in the soft ooze of the ponds; others climb about submerged plants. In pools where algae and decaying plants are in abundance, ostracods frequently swarm and appear as

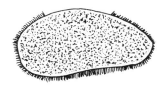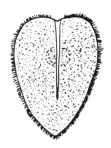

Figure 175
CYPRIS, A COMMON
OSTRACOD

countless moving specks when we look down into the water. By immersing an empty bottle and allowing the water to flow in we can collect hundreds of them.

The shell of the ostracods is heavier and less transparent than that of the water fleas. It is often sculptured or otherwise marked in patterns of contrasting colors. Many octracods are yellowish white, others are brown, orange, or violet, and those that live among algae are often green. A few species have no eyes, some have one, and still others have two.

The ostracods lay their eggs on the undersides of floating leaves and on submerged objects. The females of some species reproduce parthenogenetically, that is, they produce offspring from unfertilized eggs during the sum-

199

mer for several successive generations, and then males and female are produced in the fall. These males and females mate and produce fertilized eggs that lie dormant over the winter. In some species no males are produced at all. Depending on conditions, eggs may start developing immediately on being laid, hatching in from five to fourteen days, or they may remain dormant for a while or until such time that conditions become favorable for hatching. Young ostracods are enclosed in shells like those of their parents.

Some species of ostracods are numerous in late winter, others in early or late spring. But whatever time of the year we are sure to find them, even beneath the ice in winter, when they may be found in the bottom mud. In order to collect them at this time of the year, all we need do is scoop up some of the loose top silt from the bottom and allow it to stand in a warm place. Before long the ostracods will be seen on the surface. However, as they are too small to be seen satisfactorily with the naked eye, either a hand lens or microscope will be required.

If you want to culture ostracods as food for small aquarium animals, boil for about ten minutes two grams of whole-wheat grains and three grams of timothy hay in enough pond water to cover. Then add about a liter of filtered pond water and set aside for a few days until the bacterial decomposition has made the water alkaline. Then inoculate the culture medium with pond water containing ostracods. The culture may be maintained in a wide dish kept covered to retard evaporation but not so tightly as to exclude air. It should also be placed in sunlight that will favor the growth of algae and be kept at ordinary room temperature.

NONE OF THE animals we have discussed are found in such a variety of situations as the wheel animalcules or rotifers. They are found on the surface waters of lakes, they swarm through the shallows of ponds and bogs, they live in the cool waters of perennial springs and can exist in the most transient of pools and puddles. We can even find them in a rain barrel, a rainspout, or stone urn. Some species live in the open water in vast hosts and are called plankton rotifers, others live in the bottom ooze of plant-filled shallows, still others on the stems and leaves of plants. There are even some that live symbiotically within the tissues of water plants, and others that fashion a case or tube by cementing together little brown pellets. Some rotifers are

ADVENTURE 44

We Intrude on the Privacy of the Wheel Animalcules

quite agile and swift-moving. They feed on microscopic animals. Others, which are larger and slower, are vegetarians. There are sessil ones too; they are the ones that live in tubes.

Rotifers are mainly microscopic in size, but a few of the larger ones can be seen with the naked eye. Many have brilliant colors and sometimes are so abundant as to color the water. Most rotifers are solitary and move freely through the water, while others form colonies that are conspicuous and when attached to leaf tips may appear flowerlike. Frequently they become detached from the leaf tips and go bowling through the water like small white rolling spheres that are sufficiently large to be visible to the naked eye.

The rotifers are among the hardiest of animals and can withstand the most adverse conditions. They can survive repeated desiccation and great extremes of drought and cold. In the fall they produce tough shells and lie dormant through the winter; they can even be frozen into the ice for a long time and still be able to resume their normal activities when thawed out.

Rotifers come in an infinite variety of forms, yet all have one feature in common: circlets of cilia. Look at a rotifer under the microscope (Figure 176) and you will be surprised at its transparency. All its internal or-

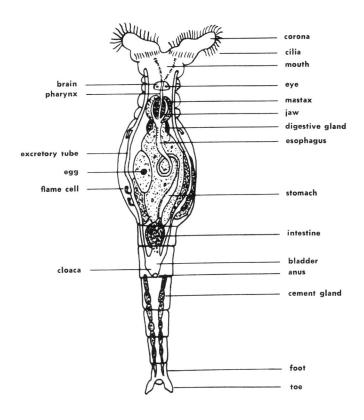

brain
pharynx

excretory tube

egg

flame cell

cloaca

corona
cilia
mouth

eye
mastax
jaw
digestive gland
esophagus

stomach

intestine

bladder
anus

cement gland

foot

toe

Figure 176
FEMALE ROTIFER

gans and what goes on inside can readily be
seen. It has no privacy. The two circlets of
cilia rim the head region, or corona, and with
hundreds of cilia beating rapidly they appear
like two rapidly rotating wheels, hence the

name Rotifera, or wheel bearers. The rotifers use the cilia for propulsion and for collecting food. The mouth is at the lower edge of the corona and opens into the pharynx, the lower end of which forms a grinding organ called the mastax.

The mastax, which is a sort of food pouch, is equipped with chitinous teeth or jaws that crush or grind food materials, such as algae or protozoa, that are swept into the mouth by the cilia. A short esophagus leads into a glandular stomach in which food is digested; in some species it is digested in both .the stomach and intestine. Undigested food particles pass into the cloaca and out through the cloacal opening (anus). The excretory system consists of two long tubes and flame cells. The tubes connect with a bladder that contracts at intervals, forcing the contents into the cloaca and thence out through the cloacal opening. The bladder also helps the animal to maintain a proper water balance.

To follow digestion in the rotifer, prepare a wheat medium by adding about one hundred pieces of seed wheat to about 100 cc. of distilled water. Heat until it comes to a boil. Boil for several minutes. Then add a few grains of Congo red. Mix well and allow solution to cool. Transfer a drop of the solution to a slide containing rotifers. The process of digestion is demonstrated by changes in the color of the dye.

At the lower extremity of the rotifer you will observe what is commonly called the foot. In some species it is forked and might better be called a tail. The animal uses it to attach itself to plants or other objects, though a cementlike substance secreted by the cement glands does the actual adhering. As male rotifers are extremely minute we do not often find them. In some species the eggs develop without fertilization, and it is a question whether males exist at all. In those spe-

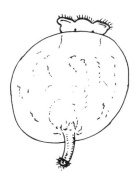

Figure 177
PTERODINA

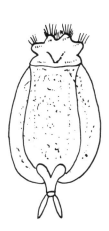

Figure 178
EUCHYLANIS

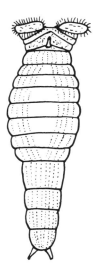

Figure 179
PHILODINA

Figure 180
MELICERTA

cies where males occur they are usually smaller than the females and degenerate.

Since rotifers possess so many fantastic forms and colors, they are among the most interesting of all freshwater animals, and you should have many interesting moments watching and studying them. Several of the commoner species are illustrated in Figures 177 to 180. Be sure to look for Melicerta (Figure 180), which is visible to the naked eye. This rotifer builds a tube that is better seen through a good hand lens. It lives on the lower surface of lily pads, hornwort, and milfoil, where it can usually be found in fairly large numbers. It is a most beautiful creature and worth every effort to find it.

ADVENTURE 45

We Marvel at Nature's Ingenuity

WE HAVE SEEN that water insects show many nice refinements for an aquatic existence, these adjustments being in the nature of structural changes. In no insect are these adaptations better illustrated than in the water scavenger beetles (Figure 181), or hydrophilids.

These elongated, elliptical black beetles are sometimes confused with the diving beetles (Adventure 40), which they resemble superficially. The hydrophilids have short, club-shaped antennae; the dytiscidae, or diving beetles, have slender, threadlike antennae. The hydrophilids can also be distinguished from the dytiscidae by their long slender palpi, which are often mistaken for antennae, and by their more convex shape. In some species there is, on the lower surface of the thorax, a sharp spine that projects backward between the legs. But we do not have to collect these beetles and examine them; we can identify them from the manner in which they hang from the surface of the water. The diving beetles hang with their heads down, the water scavenger beetles with their heads up. Before the diving beetles submerge they lift their wing covers and take in a bubble of air beneath them. The water scavenger beetles, instead of using their wing covers, extend their antennae through the surface film and with them pull back a bubble of air that spreads over the lower surface of the body like a silvery blanket.

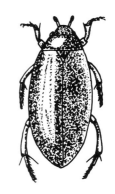

Figure 181
WATER SCAVENGER BEETLE,
HYDROUS TRIANGULARIS

The water scavenger beetles are common in quiet pools and ponds, where they may be found swimming through the water or crawling among the plants growing on the bottom. Although they feed on decaying matter, whence their name, they also live on plants and living water animals.

In their general form the beetles resemble

a boat. The smoothly elliptical contour and the polished surface of the body are admirably designed to lessen water resistance and to enable them to glide through the water easily and expeditiously. The legs, too, with the exception of the first pair, are broad and thin and fringed on the tarsi with hairs. If you want to observe how the beetles use their legs in swimming, place one of them in an aquarium or pan. The "stroke" is made by the flat surface, aided by the spreading hairs, but on the "recover" the legs are turned so as to cut the water, the hairs at the same time falling back against the tarsus from the resistance of the water as the legs are being drawn forward. Since the hind legs are nearest the center of gravity they are the chief organs of propulsion, but the second pair is also used for this purpose. The legs are used alternately in much the same sequence as land insects, a method of propulsion that gives the insects a sort of wobbling motion. The diving beetles move their hind legs simultaneously and therefore can swim in a straight line and with a greater economy of movement.

Hydrophilids are easily collected with a net and do well in an aquarium. The largest of our common species is *Hydrous triangularis* (Figure 181). It measures about an inch

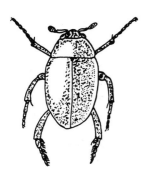

Figure 182
TROPISTERNUS

and a half long, with the ventral surface of the abdomen pubescent except for a broad, smooth streak down the middle of all but the first segment. There are also more or less distinct triangular yellow spots on the sides of the abdominal segments. A smaller species, Tropisternus (Figure 182), is shiny black. It is very common and one of the most abundant of the hydrophilids.

TURTLES may seem sluggish in their behavior when compared to other members of the reptile group, such as the snakes, for instance, which seem always to be on the alert and are quick and sinuous in their movements. But their apparent sluggishness is quite misleading. Have you ever noticed as you approached a pond how quickly a turtle, basking in the sun on a submerged log, disappeared into the water even though you walked quietly and seemingly made no noise? Turtles seem to have a keen sense of hearing, but although they have well-developed middle and inner ears, they are, as a matter of fact, poor of hearing and cannot hear in the accepted meaning of the word. At least no one as yet has shown that they are capable of responding to sound waves transmitted through the

ADVENTURE 46

We Acquire Some Pets

air. Turtles undoubtedly heard at one time, otherwise they would not have such complete ears, but somewhere in the past they began to substitute other senses for that of hearing. Present-day turtles are exceptionally sensitive to vibrations, and astonishingly slight vibrations transmitted to the skin or shell will evoke an instant response.

Turtles also have a keen sense of sight and can distinguish various colors, as you can find out by some simple experiments. Actually a turtle's range of color perception approximates our own. Certain colors, however, are more readily recognized than others. Try to find out what they are. The senses of taste and smell appear weakly developed, but apparently they function adequately, since the turtle is able to distinguish between different

Figure 183
PAINTED TURTLE

kinds of food both in and out of the water. Turtles have a fair degree of learning ability. They have been taught to distinguish between patterns of vertical and horizontal black and white lines and to follow mazes. Perhaps some simple learning experiments may suggest themselves to you.

Aquatic turtles, such as the painted and spotted species, thrive in captivity and can be kept in an aquarium containing several inches of water or in a semiaquatic terrarium described in Adventure 30. The painted turtle (Figure 183) is the commonest Eastern pond turtle and may be recognized by its comparatively smooth and somewhat flat upper shell (carapace), bright yellow bands against the black of its throat and extended head, and the crimson spots or blotches along the edges of the lower shell (plastron). The spotted turtle can be distinguished from all other turtles by the yellow spots on its black upper shell and neck. This species has been used extensively on habit formation, as mentioned above. It seems to profit by experience and to learn quite rapidly. Both turtles may be fed bits of fish, ground raw beef, liver, earthworms, sliced hard-boiled egg, lettuce, and apple slices. As they swallow their food beneath the water, it is apt to become foul and should be changed regularly.

The painted and spotted turtles occur in ponds, especially those that are partly overgrown with weeds among which they swim. Here too are found the musk turtles, mud turtles, and snapping turtles. The musk turtle, so named because it secretes a substance having a musk odor, is one of our smallest species. It is a rather unattractive turtle. It has an oval-shaped, highly arched, smooth brown upper shell and a hard, small, yellowish lower shell. The leathery folds of skin on the legs are a purple-gray color. The musk turtle is primarily a bottom forager and spends most of its time in the mud, which it matches in color. For this reason it is not a desirable aquarium or semiaquarium inhabitant, since it constantly stirs up the mud or gravel and uproots plants. Neither is the mud turtle, which is not a particularly common species. This species has a plain dull brown carapace, a broad oval, yellowish plastron, and lives in muddy bottoms. Large snapping turtles should be avoided at all times. They are mean, vicious, and dangerous. They are the largest of our freshwater turtles, some weighing forty pounds or more, and are quite impossible as pets, not only because of their snapping and biting habits, but also because of their large diet requirements.

The small turtles, those that often have gaudy designs painted on their backs and are sold in stores, also do well in captivity, but as they are Southern forms the temperature of the aquarium should be maintained at about 70° F. They can be fed the same kind of food as other turtles. The prepared foods sold in stores for turtles are of doubtful value, as they have little nourishment and

Figure 184
**PAINTED TURTLE IN
SEMIAQUATIC TERRARIUM**

213

insufficient bulk when placed on the water. The practice of painting designs on their backs is to be deplored. Aside from the fact that the turtles may suffer by this painting, the paint or enamel seriously interferes with shell growth. In keeping turtles as pets, remember that they need sunshine and should be kept where the sun will shine on them for several hours a day. Be sure, however, that they do not get baked from the sun. A stone or other object should be placed in the water so that they can bask on it (Figure 184) as well as hide under it should the sun get too strong. A few stones arranged in the form of a cave would be most acceptable. Feeding twice a week is sufficient.

ADVENTURE 47

We Arrive at the End of the Book

DURING the course of these adventures, particularly on your visits to ponds and streams, have you noticed long, slender insects with spindly legs (Figure 185) in quiet shallow inlets and pools overgrown with algae mats and duckweed? The long, thin body of the insects resembles a small twig or a filament of grass, and one glance at the legs would almost lead one to wonder how they can support the body even though it is light in weight. Should we examine one of these insects carefully, we would see that the head is as long as the entire thorax, although the thorax is long too, that the eyes are round and projecting, and that the long antennae are elbowed, or bent.

Curious as these insects may be in form, even more so is their manner of walking. Watch them the next time you see them, and observe how carefully they walk over the surface of the water or on the floating plants,

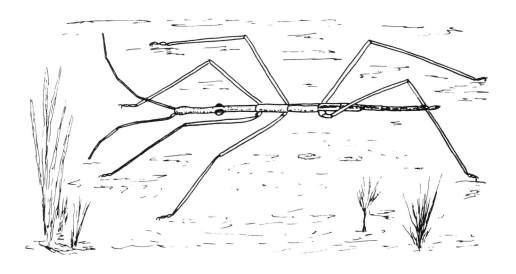

Figure 185
WATER MEASURER

215

their bodies considerably elevated. They walk with a deliberate gait as if measuring each step as they go. Hence their name, water measurers. They are also known as marsh treaders.

If you want to know what they do as they prowl among the plants, watch them for a while. Very likely you will find that they are in search of food, mosquito larvae and pupae, other water insects, and small crustaceans, which they spear with their sharp beak.

Water measurers lay their eggs from April through June. The eggs are brown and spindle-shaped and covered with a horny coating beautifully sculptured. They are laid singly and attached to cattail sprouts, grasses that grow along the margin, and other plants. About seventeen days after they are laid, the eggs hatch into young measurers that molt five times before becoming adult.

These insects do well in an aquarium and their life history is easily followed. Several precautions must be observed, however. Be careful when capturing the water measurers that you do not wrench or pull off their legs, as they are easily broken off. Also keep the level of the water in the aquarium about two or three inches from the screen-covered top. For food they can be given all kinds of small insects, dropped on the water, earthworms, mealworms, and bits of raw beef. You will find that the eggs are often attached to the sides of the aquarium.